WORLD WAR TWO:

U.S. MILITARY PLANS FOR THE INVASION OF JAPAN

TOP SECRET

WORLD WAR TWO:

U.S. MILITARY PLANS FOR THE INVASION OF JAPAN

EDITED BY THOMAS FENSCH

New Century Books

Please inquire about forthcoming books in the
TOP SECRET series:

New Century Books
P.O. Box 7113
The Woodlands, Tx., 77387-7113

Library of Congress Number: 2001117309
ISBN #:   Hardcover   0-930751-05-1
               Softcover   0-930751-06-X

CONTENTS

A Note to the Reader . . .

This volume contains over 100 pages of U.S. military files covering the final months of the war with Japan.

The military was faced with the problem of how to win the war with Japan, especially IF the atomic bomb did not work, or if it did not meet production and/or military deadlines.

These files show the McArthur/Nimitz rivalry over command control and military planners' sensitivity about confronting President Harry Truman over casualty estimates, a total estimate of at least "one quarter million" casualties, should the Allied forces storm the beaches of Japan in a Normandy-style invasion.

Documents include coverage of anticipated Japanese reaction to an invasion of southern Kyushu, details of the planned campaign against Japan (code-named Operation Olympic), cables to Potsdam regarding the A-bomb test of July 16, 1945 and instructions to General Carl Spaatz on use of the atomic bomb against a Japanese target.

This volume contains material which was previously classified secret; it was eventually declassified. These pages were reprinted from paper pages, then transferred to a CD-ROM for storage purposes. The CD-ROM was then reprocessed for electronic publishing.

The publisher assumes no responsibility for the accuracy of this material; we have attempted to be as faithful as possible to the original text. We have made no changes to the text material itself.

We also advise that there may be further items still classified secret by the government on this subject.

U.S. MILITARY PLANS
FOR THE
INVASION OF JAPAN

**Document 1: "Directive for Operation OLYMPIC."
JCS 1331/2, 14 May 1945.** This is a report prepared by the Joint Staff and sent to the Joint Chiefs of Staff (JCS). It points to issues that still had to be settled in order for agreement to be reached on a directive for the final campaign in the Pacific. The document focuses in particular on the "who is to be in charge" question.

**Document 2: "Directive for Operation OLYMPIC."
JCS 1331/3, 2S May 1945.** This is the last version of the directive for the final Pacific campaign, as dispatched to the Pacific commanders. It contains the decision on overall command of the operation. As the document indicates, a directive to prepare for the operation had already been issued to MacArthur and Nimitz on 3 April. This document is presented here, out of chronological order, because its contents are so closely related to those of document 1.

Document 3: "Japanese Reaction to An Operation Against Southern Kyushu." JIC 191/7, 16 May 1945. This was the eighth version of a report on anticipated Japanese reaction to an invasion of southern Kyushu. This version is included here because it was the latest iteration prepared prior to the dispatch of the directive discussed in documents 1 and 2 above.

This document demonstrates the consistency of the "six combat divisions, two depot divisions" projection for Japanese units on Kyushu Island by 1 November 1945. That estimate, first made more than a year earlier, formed the basis for the figures that would be given to President Truman on 18 June 1945. This projection remained in place right up to the eve of the Potsdam conference in July. The projected Japanese manpower figure for 1 November in this document was 390,000, rather than the 350,000 figure that was used in most of the previous versions of the report. (MacArthur's staff, for its part, estimated the number at 300,000.) The differences did not relate to combat strength but rather to numbers of support forces and naval and air-ground troops.

Document 4: "Details of the Campaign Against Japan." JPS 697/D, 14 June 1945. This memorandum from Admiral Leahy set up the 18 June meeting with President Truman that would review plans for bringing the war with Japan to an end. It was forwarded to the Joint Planning Staff (JPS), which directed the Joint War Plans

Committee (JWPC) to draft a response. On the document's distribution list, four of the ten names are those of members of the Joint Planning Staff—two Army and two Navy officers. One of these Army representatives, Brig. Gen. Charles Cabell, was an Army Air Force (the Air Force was then part of the US Army) officer who would later go on to serve as Deputy Director of Central Intelligence. Two other members of the JPS—Rear Adm. B.H. Bieri and Brig. Gen. J.E. Hull, the Army's Chief of Plans—were de facto co-chairmen of the JWPC.

Document 5: Details of the Campaign Against Japan. JWPC 369/1, 15 June 1945. This is the JWPC's response to the JPS request for a draft reply to Admiral Leahy's memo of 14 June. Upon receiving this document, the JPS made some modifications and submitted it to the Chiefs as JCS 1388. The JPS revisions in document 5 included deletions that has BEEN marked with brackets; the most noteworthy of these are marked on pages 51 and 53–54. This is an espe-cially important document because it demon-strates the military planners' sensitivity about confronting the President over casualty esti-mates. It does give a total estimate of roughly "a quarter of a million," which was consistent with the casualty data used by the staffs of both MacArthur and Nimitz.

Document 6: Details of the Campaign Against Japan. JCS 1388, 16 June 1945. This is the JPS version mentioned above. In addition to the deletions noted above, the "enclosure" attached at the end of this JCS paper is noteworthy. This enclosure, apparently prepared after the main draft was written, proposes further changes. One of these was language to replace the casualty estimate deleted from the JWPC version; this language offers the figures that General Hull had requested on 16 June for the 18 June meeting with the President. Hull's request presumably was prompted by the deletion of the JWPC figures and a belief on his part that, given the language of Admiral Leahy's memo, some figures had to be offered for the President.

Document 7: Memorandum for the Chief of Staff: Amplifying Details on Planners' Paper for Presentation to the President. Undated—presumably 17 or possibly 18 June 1945. Prepared by General Hull after he received the response to his request for casualty figures from various Pacific operations. This is a summary of JCS 1388 (described in document 6 above), for use by General Marshall in briefing the President at the 18 June meeting.

Document 8: Minutes of Meeting Held at the White House on Monday 18 June 1945, at 1530. Document 598 of Foreign Relations of the United States (FRUS). Diplomatic Papers: The Conference of Berlin (Potsdam Conference), 1945. Vol. I (Washington, DC, GPO 1960, pp. 902-911). General Marshall read into the record the summary offered by General Hull (document 7 above). Tables from JCS 1388 were used at the meeting. Because some disagreement persisted over the specific language of JCS 1388, the document itself was not given to the President at that time. In fact, the agreed version was not completed until 11 July, when it was included in the background papers for the Potsdam Conference.

Document 9: Proposed Changes to Details of the Campaign Against Japan. JCS 1388/1, 20 June 1945. This document shows (a) that agreement still had not been reached on JCS 1388 by the time of the 18 June meeting with Truman (prompting Gen. Hull to prepare his summary for the President) and (b) that the casualty issue continued to be debated, with Nimitz's estimates remaining close to those offered by MacArthur's staff and by the JWPC.

Document 10: Proposed Changes to Details of the Campaign Against Japan. Memorandum For The Assistant Secretary, War Department General Staff, 25 June 1945. This document shows that the Chief of Naval Operations, Admiral King, apparently supported Admiral Nimitz's recommendations. It also shows, however, that the War Department did not accept these recommendations, and that the disagreement continued at least through late June.

Document 11: Map—Estimated Japanese Dispositions on Kyushu, 21 July 1945. From MAGIC Far East Summary of 21 July (the same day the Groves report on the successful atomic bomb test arrived in Potsdam). SRS 488.

Document 12: Cables to Potsdam Regarding the A-Bomb Test of 16 July. *FRUS, Vol. II, Documents 1303,1304, and 1305, pp. 1360-1369.*

Document 13: Instruction to General Carl Spaatz on Use of the Atomic Bomb Against a Japanese Target. 25 July 1945. This document can be found in many sources. Spaatz reportedly carried it with him when he departed for the Far East on 24 July (Far East time] to take over a newly created Air Force command role. He was under instructions to deliver the document personally to MacArthur and Nimitz.

Document 14: Map—Estimated Distribution of Japanese Forces on Kyushu. 25 July 1945. From MAGIC Far East Summary on that date, SRS 492.

Document 15: Map—Estimated Disposition of Japanese Forces on Kyushu. 26 July 1945. Also attached is a table (**Document 15A)** showing estimated Japanese air strength. Both items were from the MAGIC Far East Summary of 26 July, SRS 493.

Document 16: Cable from Stimson to Truman, AGWAR Washington to Tripartite Conference, Babelsberg, Germany. 30 July 1945. This message underscored the need for President Truman's agreement on the language of a statement that would be released as soon as the atomic bomb was used. The message alerted Truman to a text being dispatched by courier that Stimson wanted the President to approve as quickly as possible. Truman, however, either misunderstood the request or consciously used the occasion to give his guidance on the dropping of the bomb itself. His handwritten message on the back of the cable said "no sooner than August 2" (i.e., after he had left Potsdam). This note was typed and sent to Stimson immediately before Truman received—later that same day—the couriered text of the public statement to which Stimson had referred in his cable. The dates of these messages have generated much misinterpretation. The records are in the Truman documents collection compiled by historian Dennis Merrill.

Document 17: Alternatives to OLYMPIC. JWPC 397, 4 August 1945. Some interesting comments were handwritten on the document by unidentified readers. One such reader wrote, "Sec'y told we non-concur." Two other handwritten notes that appeared to accompany this document reflect concern at the senior level of the military planning groups. One of these is addressed to General Lincoln, the senior Army representative on the Joint War Plans Committee. The other refers to the views of General Cabell, the Army Air Force representative on the Joint Planning Staff.

Documents: 18 and 18 A Through F: On the President's response to a query from Air Force Historian James Cate regarding Truman's role in the orders to use the atomic bomb. December 1952-January 1953. These documents are from the Truman records compiled by Dennis Merrill. They include Cate's letter of request and Truman's handwritten draft response—a personal note in which he said General Marshall had told him that the invasion would have cost "at a minimum a quarter of a million casualties."

DOCUMENT 1

J.C.S. 1331/2   COPY No. 38
14 May 1945   (SPECIAL DISTRIBUTION)
Pages 5 - 8, include.

JOINT CHIEFS OF STAFF

DIRECTIVE FOR OPERATION "OLYMPIC"
References: a. J.C.S. 1331
b. J.C.S. 1259/4
c. J.C.S. 1259/5

Note by the Secretaries

The enclosed report of the Joint Staff Planners
is submitted for consideration.

A. J. McFARLAND,
E. D. GRAVES, JR.;
Joint Secretariat.

DISTRIBUTION	COPY NO.
Admiral Leahy	1
General Marshall	2 & 5
Admiral King	3
General Arnold	4
General Handy	6
Admiral Edwards	7
Admiral Cooke	8
General Hull	9
General Kuter	10
Admiral Duncan	11
General Lindsay	12
General Lincoln	13
Captain Campbell	14
Secy., JCS	15
Secy., JPS	16
Secy., JWPC	17
Secy., JSSC	18

TOP SECRET

ENCLOSURE
DIRECTIVE FOR OPERATION "OLYMPIC"
Report by the Joint Staff Planners

1. Plans and preparations for the invasion of Japan were directed in J.C.S. 1259/4. The attached directive, prepared pursuant to J.C.S. 1331, directs the execution of these plans and preparations for the initial operation (OLYMPIC).

2. The directive (Appendix) is agreed by the Joint Staff Planners except for the wording of paragraph 1 c (1) (page 18) in which the point in question is considered of sufficient importance to call it to the attention of the Chiefs of Staff. The Navy Planners recommend the wording ". . . and will coordinate his plans with CINCAFPAC-CINCSWPA's plan for the campaign on land." The Army Planner and Army Air Forces Planner recommend the wording ". . . in conformity with CINCAFPAC-CINCSWPA's plan for the campaign on land."

3. The Army Planner and Army Air Forces Planner consider that OLYMPIC must be treated as a single, integrated operation, requiring a single primary responsibility. They believe it unsound to trust the phases of OLYMPIC as separate and distinct matters. Considering the OLYMPIC objectives, the battle in Kyushu is primary and all phases of the campaign must be built back from and must be adjusted to support this battle. Accordingly, while recognizing CINCPAC's responsibility for the naval and

amphibious phases of the campaign, they believe that the conduct of these phases should be in conformity with CINCAFPAC's over-all plan. They consider that their wording does not take away from CINCPAC any power of decision which is inherent in his responsibility. It is clearly recognized and standard practice that in joint operations the Army commander must obtain concurrence of the Navy commander in the landing areas and in those portions of his battle plan which involve the Navy.

Abbreviations: CINCAFPAC—Commander   in Chief, U.S. Army Forces, Pacific
CINCSSWPA—Commander   in   Chief, Southwest Pacific Area
CINCPAC—Commander in Chief, U.S. Pacific Fleet
CINCPOA—Commander   in   Chief, Pacific Ocean Areas

4. The Navy Planners consider that adequate integration of the phases of the OLYMPIC operation is assured by directing Admiral Nimitz to "coordinate his plans" for the naval and amphibious phases with General MacArthur's plan for the campaign in Kyushu and to "cooperate with and assist CINCAFPAC in his plans and preparations . . . etc." (paragraph 1 c) (2)). The Navy Planners recognize that plans and preparations must be built back from the land campaign plan adopted, and that the plans for the naval and amphibious phases of the campaign must take account of and support the plans for the land campaign. They consider also, however, that the

19

land campaign adopted must be one that fits in with the practical aspects and possibilities of the amphibious operations. They do not consider that the wording of the subparagraph in question, proposed by the Army Planner and Army Air Forces Planner provides for the adjustment of the plans of each commander to those of the other, in accordance with the terms of the directive for plans and preparations for the invasion of Japan set up in J.C.S. 1259/4 (Enclosure "B", subparagraph a (6) and b (4)) which directive was made pursuant to the general provisions of Enclosure "A", J.C.S. 1259/4, was agreed by the Joint Staff Planners and by the Joint Chiefs of Staff, and accepted by the commanders in the field, and according to which plans and preparations are proceeding. They feel that the effect of the wording proposed by the Army Planner and Army Air Forces Planner would be to remove from Admiral Nimitz all controls as to decision on a plan for the success of which he is responsible.

RECOMMENDATION
5. That the Joint Chiefs of Staff decide the point of difference in subparagraph 1 c (2) of the attached directive and issue the directive immediately.

APPENDIX

DRAFT

DIRECTIVE TO CINCAFPAC-CINCSWPA, CINCPAC-CINCPOA, AND CG, 20TH AIR FORCE

1. Pursuant to and in furtherance of directives contained in J.C.S. 1259/4 and J.C.S. 1259/5, the following directive is issued and is effective on receipt:

a. The Joint Chiefs of Staff direct the invasion of Kyushu (operation OLYMPIC), target date 1 November 1945, in order to;

(1) Intensify the blockade and aerial bombardment of Japan,

(2) Contain and destroy major enemy forces,

(3) Support further advances,

for the purpose of establishing the conditions favorable to the decisive invasion of the industrial heart of Japan.

b. CINCAFPAC-CINCSWPA:

(1) Is charged with the responsibility for the conduct of the campaign in Kyushu.

(2) Will make plans and preparations for the continuance of the campaign in Japan and cooperate with CINCPAC in the plans and preparations for the naval and amphibious phases thereof.

c. CINCPAC-CINCPOA:

(1) Is charged with the responsibility for the conduct of the naval and amphibious phases of the OLYMPIC operation,

(Navy) . . . and will coordinate his plans with CINCAFPAC-CINCSWPA's plan for the campaign

21

on land.

(Army) . . . in conformity with CINCAFPAC-CINCSWPA's plan for the campaign on land.

(2) Will cooperate with and assist CINCAFPAC in his plans and preparations for the campaign in Japan.

d. The Commanding General, Twentieth Air Force will cooperate in the plans, preparations and execution of operation OLYMPIC and in the continuance of the campaign in Japan. At appropriate times, to be determined by the Joint Chiefs of Staff, the Twentieth Air Force will come under the direction of the appropriate commander for the support of operations directed above.

DOCUMENT 2

J.C.S. 1331/3   COPY NO. 24
25 May 1945   (SPECIAL DISTRIBUTION
Pages 9-10, incl.

JOINT CHIEFS OF STAFF
DIRECTIVE FOR OPERATION "OLYMPIC"
Note by the Secretaries

By informal action on 25 May 1945 the Joint
Chiefs of Staff approved the enclosed directive
which was dispatched the same day.

A. J. McFARLAND,
E. D. GRAVES, JR.,
Joint Secretariat.

DISTRIBUTION   COPY NO.

Admiral Leahy   1
General Marshall   2 & 5
Admiral King   3 & 6
General Arnold   4
General Handy   7

Admiral Edwards	8
Admiral Cooke	9
General Hull	10
General Kuter	11
Admiral Duncan	12
General Lindsay	13
General Lincoln	14
Captain Campbell	15
Secy., JCS	16
Secy., JPS	17
Secy., JWPC	18
Secy., JSSC	19

ENCLOSURE

DIRECTIVE
TO
COMMANDER IN CHIEF, U.S. ARMY FORCES,
PACIFIC COMMANDER IN CHIEF, U.S. PACIFIC
FLEET COMMANDING GENERAL, TWENTIETH
AIR FORCE

1. Pursuant to and in furtherance of directives contained in WAR 62773 and WAR 62774, dated 3 April 1945 (J.C.S. 1259/4 and J.C.S. 1259/5), the following directive is issued and is effective on receipt:

a. The Joint Chiefs of Staff direct the invasion of Kyushu (Operation OLYMPIC), target date 1 November 1945, in order to:

(1) Intensify the blockade and aerial bombardment of Japan,

(2) Contain and destroy major enemy forces,

(3) Support further advances,

for the purpose of establishing the conditions favorable to the decisive invasion of the industrial heart of Japan.

b. CINCAFPAC-CINCSWPA:

(1) Is charged with the primary responsibility for the conduct of operation OLYMPIC including control, in case of exigencies, of the actual amphibious assault through the appropriate naval commander.

(2) Will make plans and preparations for the continuance of the campaign in Japan and cooperate with CINCPAC in the plans and preparations for the naval and amphibious phases thereof.

c. CINCPAC-CINCPOA:

(1) Is charged with the responsibility for the conduct of the naval and amphibious (subject to paragraph 1 b (1) above) phases of the OLYMPIC operation, and will correlate his plans with CINCAFPAC-CINCSWPA.

(2) Will cooperate with and assist CINCAFPAC in his plans and preparations for, and the conduct of, the campaign in Japan.

d. The land campaign and requirements therefor are primary in the OLYMPIC operation. Account of this will be taken in the preparation, coordination and execution of plans.

e. COMMANDING GENERAL, TWENTIETH AIR FORCE, will cooperate in the plans, preparations, and execution of operation OLYMPIC and in the continuance of the campaign in Japan. At appropriate times, to be determined by the Joint Chiefs of Staff, the Twentieth Air Force will come under the direction of the appropriate commander for the support of operations directed above.

DOCUMENT 3

TOP SECRET   COPY NO. 31
J.I.C. 191/7   (LIMITED DISTRIBUTION)
16 May 1945

JOINT INTELLIGENCE COMMITTEE
(Service Members)

JAPANESE REACTIONS TO AN OPERATION
AGAINST SOUTHERN KYUSHU
References: a J.I.S. 158/M
b. J.I.C. 191/5

Note by the Secretary

The enclosed revision of J.I.C. 191/5, prepared
by the Service Members of the Joint Intelligence
Staff in response to reference a, is submitted for
informal consideration by the Service Members of
the Joint Intelligence Committee.
Copies of this paper are being forwarded by the
Joint War Plans Committee as a preliminary
response, pending consideration by the Service
Members of the Joint Intelligence Committee.

JAMES S. LAY, JR.,
Secretary.

DISTRIBUTION   COPY NO.

Director of Naval Intelligence   1 & 7
Assistant Chief of Staff, G-2   2 & 8
Assistant Chief of Air Staff,
    Intelligence   3 & 9
File (Col. Peck)   4
Secy, JCS   5
Secy, JIS   6, 10-20
Secy, JWPC   21-27
Secy, JSSC   28
Secy, JPS   29
Asst. Chief of Air Staff, Plans   30
Chief, Strat. And Policy Group, OPD 31

TOP SECRET

ENCLOSURE

JAPANESE REACTION TO AN OPERATION
AGAINST SOUTHERN KYUSHU
Report by the Service Members, Joint
Intelligence Committee

STATEMENT OF THE PROBLEM

1. To estimate Japanese capabilities and reaction to an assault on southern Kyushu about 1 November 1945.

ASSUMPTIONS

2. a. We have consolidated our present positions in the Philippines, Ryukyus and Bonins.

b. The U.S.S.R. has entered the war against Japan simultaneously with or shortly before the Kyushu assault.

DISCUSSION AND CONCLUSIONS

3 General. The Japanese appreciate that from our present positions we will have the capability of major attack against Japan or China. Our occupation of islands in the Ryukyus intensifies their concern regarding the security of the Japanese homeland itself, and, from this time onward, primary consideration will be given to the strengthening of home defenses. However, in view of the Soviet threat, strengthening of ground forces in the homeland will not be made at the net expense of Manchuria. Soviet entry in the war simultaneously with or prior to our assault on Kyushu will cause no appreciable shifting of strength between the continent and Japan Proper.

The Japanese know that successful Allied lodgement in Kyushu would result in effective interdiction of communications between Kyushu, Honshu, Shikoku, and the Continent. Therefore, the Japanese will use all available ground, sea, and air forces to resist a landing on Kyushu and will defend desperately to prevent Allied consolidation on the island.

4. Ground. (See Appendix "A".) We estimate that at the time of Allied assault, 6 divisions plus 2 depot divisions plus army troops, making a total of about 390,000 men, would be deployed in

Kyushu. Of this number a total of about 150,000 would be initially available in southern Kyushu. Substantial reinforcements would be immediately available from other nearby areas, but the Japanese capability for bringing in such reinforcements would depend upon Allied success in isolating the battle area.

5. Air. (See Appendix "B".) We estimate that by 1 November 1945 the Japanese air forces will have a maximum total strength of 2,300 combat aircraft in tactical units. In addition there may be some 1,200 combat type aircraft in operational training units and between 1,500 and 2,000 specially equipped non-combat trainer type aircraft might be available for suicide operations. Enemy air reactions would be extremely aggressive and suicide air attacks would be employed on a lavish scale. Taking all factors into consideration we believe that a maximum of 400 to 500 bomber and fighter sorties could be launched against us during any 24-hour period. Such a maximum effort would prove to be of short duration, capable of repetition on a declining scale following intervals of temporary recuperation. We now consider it possible that the enemy might continue his air effort against us in the Kyushu area until his air forces have been largely dissipated. Soviet entry into the war at this time probably would have no effect upon initial air reaction but would reduce further the enemy's capability for bringing in replacements.

6. Naval. (See Appendix "C".) Battleships, cruisers, and destroyers which are still operational at the time would probably be organized into sui-

cide task forces and would endeavor to sortie in a desperate effort to oppose our landings. Submarines, midget-submarines, suicide and small surface craft would be employed in large numbers, but should offer no serious problem. Extensive minefields will probably be encountered.

TOP SECRET

APPENDIX "A"
GROUND

1. General. Our operations in the Ryukyus and the Bonins has served as a warning to the Japanese of our impending attack on Japan Proper. However, though this is their primary concern, they cannot overlook the possibility of our assault upon the China Coast or the possibility of Soviet operations in Manchuria. Therefore, the Japanese will be forced to disperse their strength somewhat to counter all threats. Faced with the mounting Allied threat from the Pacific, the Japanese are currently engaged in strengthening the defenses of the Home Islands by the formation of new divisions and by limited withdrawals from the Continent. Most of these latter units seem destined for Kyushu which the Japanese appear to consider the most likely target for an initial Allied assault on Japan Proper.

Soviet entry in the war simultaneously with or prior to our assault in Kyushu will cause no appreciable shifting of strength between the Continent and Japan Proper, since the Japanese will have already apportioned their forces between those two areas in accordance with their capabilities and estimated needs. Increased Allied air action prior to and following successful lodgment in Kyushu will reduce greatly Japanese capability to reinforce Japan from the Continent, even if troops can be spared in the face of Soviet threat or pressure. We consider it probable, therefore, that the troops in the Japanese Islands on D-day will be the only ones available for use against invading Allied forces.

2. Strength and dispositions. We believe current formations of new units plus transfers from the Continent will make the following forces available in Japan Proper (including Karafutu and the Kuriles) by 1 November 1945:

Active Divs.	Depot Divs.	Total Divs.	Strength
32	14	46	2,000,000

Of this strength we estimate that 6 active divisions, 2 depot divisions, plus army troops, or a total of about 390,000 men, will be located in Kyushu.

Divisional strength in Kyushu will probably be about equally divided between the areas lying north and south of the Sammyaku range. The principal supply and depot establishments, however, as well as important areas requiring the principal antiaircraft defenses, lie in the north. Therefore, a greater personnel strength will be located in that area. Independent beach defense units and home guards, backed by divisional units, will be deployed to cover the principal landing beaches.

In additional to the regular armed forces, about 250,000 able bodied men of military age would be available in southern Kyushu for industry, agriculture, and assistance to the armed forces. About half of this number would be reservists with some military training and could be used as lightly armed home guard forces.

3. Reinforcement capabilities. Reinforcements

probably would begin moving to Kyushu as soon as it became evident that the island was the object of a major attack. The rapidity of movement would depend upon logistical considerations and Allied effectiveness in interdiction of reinforcement routes.

Some 6 divisions could be made available initially from other parts of Japan for transfer to Kyushu without seriously depleting other areas of Japan Proper.

Reinforcements could begin arriving in Kyushu from Honshu on D plus 2. Thereafter, reinforcements could arrive at the rate of about 1/2 division per day; and, provided communications with Honshu were maintained, they would continue to do so until about 10 to 12 divisions were deployed on the island. Because of the nature of the terrain and the probable effective interdiction of communications, we believe that this number of divisions is the maximum number of troops that the Japanese could employ tactically against us in sustained action. The Japanese would make every effort to maintain this strength throughout the operations.

4. <u>Japanese reactions.</u> The Japanese would resist an attack on Kyushu to the limit of their capability. We believe that initial opposition would consist of small units in well prepared beach defenses. These forces would be built up quickly to the strength of a division and might be increased to 3 to 4 divisions within a period of 5 days and to a strength of 10 to 12 active divisions by D plus 14. Of these, we believe about 8 divisions would be committed against our forces

in southern Kyushu. This number would be maintained until the Japanese capability for replacement of casualties was severely reduced by Allied interdiction of the routes leading to southern Kyushu. Divisions not committed to the action in the south would be held in reserve north of the Sammyaku Range.

APPENDIX "B"

AIR

1. General. Analysis of recent operations of the Japanese air forces suggests that the Japanese may have decided that continued suicide attack against our shipping constitutes their only capability for preventing, or at least delaying, an invasion of the Home Islands. They seem to be sacrificing their present and potential air strength in this effort and may hope by such action to forestall invasion of Japan Proper. It would seem unlikely, however, that the Japanese will continue this policy, except in the defense of the homeland, after we have established adequate land based air units in the Ryukyus and our major task force units have been withdrawn from the area.

2. Overall strength and dispositions. Even if the Japanese should endeavor to conserve and increase their air strength during the period after we have secured our main objectives in the Ryukyus, they will not be able to avoid continuing attrition of aircraft as well as continued heavy damage to their aircraft industry, maintenance and repair facilities. We estimate that as of

1 November 1945 overall strength of combat aircraft in tactical units will total about 2300 aircraft disposed approximately as follows:

Kyushu—W. Honshu—Shikoku	300
Central Honshu	400
East Honshu	700
N. Honshu—Hokkaido-Kuriles	300
Manchuria—Korea—N. China	400
Elsewhere	200
TOTAL	2300

By 1 November 1945 practically all Japanese air strength south of Shanghai will be dissipated or recalled to the northern areas. Airfields in Kyushu will have been largely neutralized but a total of some 300 aircraft probably would continue to be based on this island and on adjacent airfields in Shikoku and western Honshu.

In addition to this combat strength in tactical units, overall strength of combat types in operational training units may amount to some 1,200 aircraft, of which number perhaps 50% will be located in Japan Proper. A large proportion of these aircraft will be made available for suicide attacks, and, in addition, there may be available between 1,500 and 2,000 biplane, monoplane, and seaplane trainers equipped for carrying bombs and possessing limited capabilities in suicide operations.

3. Initial reaction. Our pre-invasion air offensive will be reinforced by substantial land-based air strength in the Ryukus, and hence should be more effective than in previous operations where

dependence has been placed upon carrier strikes alone. By the time our landing operations are actually undertaken, the airfields on Kyushu should be neutralized except for difficult staging operations. In addition, the effectiveness of enemy air operations from nearby bases in Korea, Honshu, and Shikoku should be considerably reduced by our pre-invasion air attacks. We believe, therefore, that in the early stages of our landing operations the enemy will be unable to launch against our invasion forces more than 400-500 sorties during any 24-hour period. Initial reaction would be extremely aggressive and suicide attacks would be employed on a lavish scale. The scale and effectiveness of such suicide attacks will be limited not only by the availability of aircraft and pilots, but also by the availability of an air cover of sufficient size and effectiveness to get the suicide aircraft through to their targets. The employment of Baka bombs will be limited by their dependence upon suitable launching aircraft and orthodox air cover.

4. Reinforcement capabilities and subsequent reaction. Reinforcements would be brought in rapidly from all adjacent areas; but because of reduced servicing and maintenance facilities and lack of reserves, we consider it unlikely that such reinforcements could do more than provide temporary replacements for the heavy losses likely to be incurred. At no subsequent period will the total reaction be likely to exceed the initial capability of 400-500 sorties in a 24-hour period. Such an all-out effort could not be maintained for any length of time, but we may expect, as in the

Ryukyus, recurring attacks of this nature following intervals of recuperation. We now consider it
possible that the Japanese would continue such
attacks against our shipping until their tactical
units as well as training units had been largely
dissipated and without regard for conserving
strong air strength even for the defense of the
Tokyo area.

5. Effects of Soviet entry into war. If the
U.S.S.R. should enter the war simultaneously
with or shortly before the Kyushu assault, we do
not believe there would be any substantial difference in the initial air reaction to our operation.
There would be some reduction in the reinforcements available for replacement purposes as air
strength in Korea, North China, and Manchuria
might be committed entirely against the U.S.S.R.
In general, the enemy would be compelled to commit the bulk of his air strength against us and
leave opposition to the U.S.S.R. primarily to
ground forces.

APPENDIX "C"
NAVAL

1. During the past year the Japanese Navy
has sustained severe losses in combatant ships,
bases, and personnel, resulting in the retirement
of the bulk of their combatant ships to home
waters, particularly in the Inland Sea. Some units
are believed to be in the Sasebo area.

2. The present strength plus future completion
of combatant units as of 1 November 1945 with-

<u>out allowance for attrition</u> is estimated to be as follows:

BB	CV	CVL	CVE	CA	CL	DD (1500-2300)	DD (1000)	SS
4	4	3	4	5-6	2	23	34	86

Of the strength shown above, three heavy cruisers and one large destroyer are in the Singapore area and their return to Empire waters is problematical. In addition, it is doubtful that the enemy would employ such carriers as might be available for defense of southern Kyushu, since the limited sphere of operations permits the more effective use of carrier air squadrons from land bases.

3. The battleships, cruisers, and destroyers then operational would probably be organized into suicide task forces and would attempt to sortie in a desperate effort to oppose our landings. Such opposition should be quickly eliminated by Allied air and naval power. This sortie could be from the Inland Sea through the Straits of Shimonoseki or the Bungo Straits, or even through Kii Channel, permitting in any case timely detection and interception by our forces.

4. The Japanese Navy will depend primarily upon its shore defenses (fixed and mobile artillery), submarines, midget submarines, suicide and small surface craft to protect the southern Kyushu area from amphibious attack. These should offer no serious problem, however, judging from their ineffectiveness on past occasions.

5. The waters off the Kyushu beaches are mineable to a considerable degree. The harbor entrances and bays are easily mined and are

probably already so protected. The exposed beaches could be protected by mines but to do so would require a large number to cover a long coast line. The beach gradings are suitable for considerable mining, the 100 fathom curve being from 5 to 8 miles off the coast. At the present time we have reliable information that the Japanese have minefields in the waters of Kagoshima Wan, Tanega Shima Strait, and Osumi Strait; and we may expect additional mining on an extensive scale prior to our assault.

TOP SECRET   COPY NO. 31
22 May 1945   (LIMITED DISTRIBUTION)

JOINT INTELLIGENCE COMMITTEE
(Service Members)

DECISION AMENDING J.I.C. 191/7

JAPANESE REACTIONS TO AN OPERATION
AGAINST SOUTHERN KYUSHU
Note by the Secretary

The Service Members of the Joint Intelligence Committee have by informal action approved J.I.C. 191/7, subject to minor amendments which have been incorporated in the revised pages attached hereto, and the following additional amendments:

Page 3, Line 11 -
Before "units" insert the word "latter".

Page 3, Line 18 -
Before "estimated needs", insert "capabilities and".

Page 4, Line 14 -
Change "1,000,000" to read "250,000".

Page 9, paragraph 2 -
In the tabulation, under "CA",
change "6-7" to read "5-6".

Page 9, paragraph 2 -
In the first line following the tabulation, change "four heavy cruisers" to read "three heavy cruisers".

All holders of J.I.C. 191/7 are requested to make the above changes and to substitute the attached revisions, destroying the superseded pages by burning.

JAMES S. LAY, JR,
Secretary.

DOCUMENT 4

J.P.S. 697/D   (SPECIAL DISTRIBUTION)
14 June 1945

JOINT STAFF PLANNERS
DIRECTIVE
DETAILS OF THE CAMPAIGN AGAINST JAPAN
Reference: a. SM-2140
Note by the Secretaries

The enclosure has been referred to the Joint Staff Planners for preparation of a draft memorandum for presentation to the President. It is desired that the draft memorandum be submitted to the Joint Chiefs of Staff not later than 1800, 16 June 1945.

C. H. DONNELLY,
F. J. GREEN,
Joint Secretariat.

DISTRIBUTION   COPY NO.

Rear Admiral D. B. Duncan, USN   1
Brig. General C. P. Cabell, USA   2
Brig. General G. A. Lincoln, USA   3-4
Captain Colin Campbell, USN   5
Secretary, J.P.S.   6-7
Maj. General J. E. Hull, USA   8
Secretariat, J.W.P.C.   9
File (Exec. Sec., J.C.S.)   10
Rear Admiral B. H. Bieri, USN   11
Asst. Chief of Air Staff (Plans)   12
ENCLOSURE

THE WHITE HOUSE
WASHINGTON
14 June 1945

URGENT - IMMEDIATE ACTION

MEMORANDUM FOR THE JOINT CHIEFS OF
STAFF:

The President today directed me to inform the Joint Chiefs of Staff that he wishes to meet with the Chiefs of Staff in the afternoon of the 18th, in his office, to discuss details of our campaign against Japan.

He expects at this meeting to be thoroughly informed of our intentions and prospects in preparation for his discussions with Churchill and Stalin.

He will want information as to the number of men of the Army and ships of the Navy that will be necessary to defeat Japan.

He wants an estimate of the time required and an estimate of the losses in killed and wounded that will result from an invasion of Japan proper.

He wants an estimate of the time and the losses that will result from an effort to defeat Japan by isolation, blockade, and bombardment by sea and air forces.

He desires to be informed as to exactly what we want the Russians to do.

He desires information as to what useful contribution, if any, can be made by other Allied nations.

It is his intention to make his decisions on the campaign with the purpose of economizing to the maximum extent possible in the loss of American lives.

Economy in the use of time and in money cost is comparatively unimportant.

I suggest that a memorandum discussion of the above noted points be prepared in advance for delivery to the President at the time of the meeting in order that he may find time later to study the problem.

/s/ WILLIAM D. LEAHY

DOCUMENT 5

J.W.P.C. 369/9   COPY NO. 3
15 June 1945   (SPECIAL DISTRIBUTION

JOINT WAR PLANS COMMITTEE

DETAILS OF THE CAMPAIGN AGAINST JAPAN
References: a. J.P.S. 697/D.
b. J.P.S. Memo Directive
of 14 June 1945.

Note by the Secretaries

1. The Joint War Plans Committee recommends that the enclosed memorandum be presented to the President at his conference with the
Joint Chiefs of Staff.
2. The Joint War Plans Committee has
assumed that the questions brought up by the
President will be answered and discussed orally
at the conference, and that the purpose of the
memorandum is for the President to have available an aide memoire which he could examine at

his convenience and possibly use at the forthcoming tripartite conferences.
3. Representatives of the Joint Intelligence Staff
have been consulted in the preparation of this
report.

J. T. HILLIS,
C. C. GOODE,
JOINT SECRETARIES.

DISTRIBUTION   COPY NO.

Admiral D. B. Duncan   1-2
General G. A. Lincoln   3-4
General C. P. Cabell   5,16
Captain Colin Campbell   6
Secretary, J.P.S.   7
Secretary, J.W.P.C.   8-12

ENCLOSURE

MEMORANDUM FOR THE PRESIDENT:
Subject: Campaign against Japan.

1. Strategy. Throughout the series of staff conferences with the British, we have agreed that
the over-all concept for the prosecution of the
war included provision "to bring about at the earliest possible date the unconditional surrender of
Japan." We believe that the only sure way, and
certainly the quickest way to force the surrender
of Japan is to defeat her armies on the main
Japanese islands. Hence, at recent staff confer-

ences we have proposed—and the British have agreed—that the over-all objective of the Japanese war is "to force the unconditional surrender of Japan by (1) lowering Japanese ability and will to resist by establishing sea and air blockades, conducting intensive air bombardment and destroying Japanese air and naval strength; (2) invading and seizing objectives in the industrial heart of Japan."

Since "unconditional surrender" is foreign to the Japanese nature, it is by no means certain that a formal acknowledgment thereof by a Japanese government will be recognized by Japanese armies everywhere. If, following such an acknowledgment, her armies elsewhere do not surrender, their position will be so seriously wakened as to facilitate their defeat in detail. However, the possibility must be faced that the Japanese armies everywhere must be defeated.

2. Presently planned campaign. Our agreed concept of operations for the main effort in the Pacific war is:

"Following the Okinawa operation to seize additional positions to intensify the blockade and air bombardment of Japan in order to create a situation favorable to:

"An assault on Kyushu for the purpose of further reducing Japanese capabilities by containing and destroying major enemy forces and further intensifying the blockade and air bombardment in order to establish a tactical condition favorable to:

"The decisive invasion of the industrial heart of Japan through the Tokyo Plain."

Our campaign plans have therefore been

designed to seize positions progressively closer to the Tokyo Plain—the political, industrial and communication center of Japan—with a view to isolating the Japanese islands and providing sufficient bases from which, by sea and air bombardment, conditions will be created which will make ultimate invasion of the Tokyo Plain acceptable and feasible. We have also endeavored so to design the campaign that the Japanese cannot fail to see and feel the results of is rapidly increasing tempo and magnitude, with the thought that at some stage of the campaign they will admit defeat in order to avoid further destruction.

Thus far in this campaign we have seized and developed air and naval bases in the Marinas, Iwo Jima, the Philippines and Okinawa. No further operations in the Ryukyus after completion of the Okinawa campaign are now contemplated; all available resources are being utilized to develop air and naval bases in Okinawa to maximum capacity by November 1945. By then it is expected to have about 2700 land-based aircraft operating from this area and to have completed an advanced fleet base and anchorage. The map, Tab "A", shows the land-based aircraft expected to be based within range of Japan by that time and the areas they can reach. Meanwhile every effort is also being made to transport to the Pacific from Europe the added means estimated to be required for a rapid and decisive campaign. In general the units needed to build the required bases are being moved first, followed by the required additional combat units, air and ground.

Already we have eliminated practically all Japanese sea traffic between their main islands and points to the southward of Shanghai, and severely restricted her traffic to Shanghai and Yellow Sea ports. By November 1945, when air operations from Okinawa are in full swing, there should remain to the Japanese only those sea routes across Tshushima Strait to Korea and across the Sea of Japan. It should be noted that our air and submarines are already operating in these areas on a limited scale. By November 1945 the Japanese situation is expected to be critical; their fleet units in home waters have already been so reduced as to no longer consti-tute a strategic factor; their air arm is already committing training planes to combat and will probably continue to concentrate on maximum suicide tactics; their ability to move ground forces to Japan from Asia or vice versa is already strictly reduced. The map, Tab "D", shows the estimated Japanese dispositions of ground and air forces about 1 November 1945.

In order to obtain bases still closer to the Tokyo Plain from which to augment sea and air bombardment, complete the isolation of the main Japanese islands and to provide direct air cover and support for the invasion of the Tokyo Plain, should that prove necessary, we have directed General MacArthur and Admiral Nimitz to invade southern Kyushu about 1 November 1945.

We have not yet directed the execution of any operations after the invasion of southern Kyushu, feeling that decision would better await further developments. However, plans and preparations are being made to invade the Tokyo Plain—the political, industrial and communication center of Japan—about 4 months after the southern Kyushu operation, or about 1 March 1946. We consider that this operation should be decisive. By planning and preparing for a supreme operation of this magnitude, we shall be in a position to undertake any lesser operation should developments warrant.

In the period prior to the planned invasion of the Tokyo Plain, every effort will be made to exploit the blockade and bombardment of Japan. In this period, from bases presently and prospectively available, more bombs will be dropped on Japan than were delivered against Germany during the entire European war. If the blockade and bombardment concept is capable of achieving decisive results, these will, in all probability, be brought about by this scale of effort prior to the planned date for the invasion of the Tokyo Plain. However, in the event this invasion is not considered feasible and acceptable on the planned date, a course of action to extend bombardment and blockade is open to us.

3. Examination of the map, Tab "A", shows that bases on the Asiatic mainland other than in Korea are too distant to be of value in augmenting the sea and air bombardment of Japan and in cutting the remaining Japanese sea routes across Tsushima Strait and the Sea of Japan. Furthermore, the blockade of the Yellow Sea and the sea areas to the southward is now virtually effective. There is also the likelihood that any operation in China, with its vast area and num-

bers of Japanese ground forces, will develop into a vacuum requiring ever more and more U.S. forces. We therefore discarded, as unnecessary and diversionary, operations to seize additional bases on the China coast. The best areas from which to complete the isolation of Japan are obviously either in Korea or in the southwestern part of the Japanese Archipelago. We considered three possibilities: Korea, the northwestern part of Kyushu, and southern Kyushu. Tabs "F" and "G" show the salient facts and estimates for campaigns in Korea and northwestern Kyushu.

We discarded Korea as a possible operation to follow Okinawa because of its longer sea approach, the paucity of good beaches and exits therefrom, the rugged terrain back of the beaches, the few airfield sites available for development after seizure, and the greater reinforcement capabilities of the Japanese from their fine and as yet untouched army in northern China; further, we would have difficulty both in interfering by air action with the arrival of these reinforcements and in providing adequate air cover and support to the assault because of the distance to Okinawa bases. The campaign is estimated to require about the same commitment of forces as for the invasion of southern Kyushu (14 divisions, 766,700 men).

Similarly we discarded northwestern Kyushu as a possible objective area following Okinawa because the sea approaches to the best landing area are restricted, well fortified and heavily mined; and because of Japanese capability to reinforce the area from two directions—from southern Kyushu and from Honshu. The forces required for such an operation are estimated to be in excess of those for southern Kyushu. The operation may, however, prove desirable as a development and exploitation of the landing in southern Kyushu, when it is estimated that it could be done with 12 divisions (510,000 men).

The seizure of southern Kyushu has been directed because:

a. Its occupation is essential to, and will materially further, the isolation of Japan from Korea and the mainland of Asia;

b. It is the most logical extension of our operations in the Ryukyus, since shore-based tactical air support can be furnished from Okinawa and lines of communication are shorter than for any other practicable objective;

c. Airfields on which to base approximately 40 groups (over 2,000 aircraft) can be developed, from which the air bombardment of the remainder of Japan can be greatly intensified in preparation for the invasion of Honshu, should this prove to be necessary;

d. It will contribute toward the defeat of Japanese armies in the Japanese homeland;

e. It may well prove to be the decisive operation which will terminate the war.

4. As to other areas, Admiral Mountbatten in the Southeast Asia Command plans to seize a position in the Port Swettenham-Port Dixon area on the Malay Peninsula in the latter half of August 1945 and to follow this up with a campaign to recapture Singapore beginning probably in December-January. General Wedemeyer has

advised that, in China, the Generalissimo plans to launch an overland advance with Chinese forces on the Canton-Hong Kong area beginning about 1 September 1945 and to follow up any Japanese withdrawals northward along the railroad route in central China.

5. Plans for the period after the invasion of the Tokyo Plain cannot be made with firmness at this time. If the Japanese continue to resist, plans must provide for further operations in the main islands and for possible operations on the mainland of Asia. We hope that U.S. commitments on the mainland can be kept to a minimum, with maximum effort by the Chinese, and by the Russians if they should enter the war. Hence, plans provide for continued U.S. aid to Chinese forces, the scale of which can probably be materially increased later in the campaign. Should the Japanese unconditionally surrender or concede defeat during the campaign in Japan proper, there will still remain the sizable task of disarming their forces everywhere, assembling them at ports, and returning them to their home islands.

6. Forces required for presently planned campaign. Estimates of the forces required to execute the invasion of southern Kyushu and of the Tokyo Plain are shown on the map, Tab "E". The maps, Tabs "B" and "C", show the deployment of land-based aircraft planned upon the completion of each of these two operations. The ultimately expected coverage of the Asiatic mainland and sea routes thereto is of note.

For the campaign as planned through the invasion of the Tokyo Plain, it is expected there will be in the Pacific theaters, India-Burma and china by the spring of 1946 a total of 39 Army divisions and 127 Army Air groups (8512 land-based aircraft) or a grand total in Army forces of about 3,000,000 men. General MacArthur has indicated that if operations are necessary after the invasion of the Tokyo Plain, plans should provide for the movement of additional divisions from the U.S. to the Pacific at a rate of about 4 additional divisions per month, up to the limit of a planned strategic reserve of 17 divisions.

By 1 March 1946 the following number of major combat ships are scheduled to be fully operational in the Pacific Fleet:

10 BB	26 CA
13 OBB	33 CL
2 CB	8 CL (AA)
22 CV	364 DD
2 CVB	326 DE
9 CVL	189 SS
74 CVE (43 combat)	

The above figures make no allowance for attrition. Three months after the Kyushu operation it is estimated that approximately 10% will either have been lost or still undergoing repairs to damage received in this operation. Of the operational ships in service 75% will normally be constantly available for any single operation. Others will be either undergoing operational repairs or be otherwise employed.

It is estimated that approximately 3,818 carrier-based aircraft will be available on 1 March 1946.

*End bracket missing.

7. Casualties. The cost in casualties of the main operations against Japan are not subject to accurate estimate. The scale of Japanese resistance in the past has not been predictable. Casualty expectancy rates based on experience in the Pacific vary greatly from the short bloody battle of Tarawa to the unopposed landing at Lingayen. It would be difficult to predict whether Jap resistance on Kyushu would more closely resemble the fighting on Okinawa or whether it would parallel the battle of Leyte.

Certain general conclusions can, however, be reached. The highest casualty rate occurs during the assault phase of an amphibious operation; casualties in land warfare are a function of the length of campaign and of the scale of opposition encountered. Naval casualties can be expected to vary directly with the number of amphibious operations involved and with the length of the campaign. Casualties can be kept to a minimum, then, by terminating the war at the earliest possible time by means of the fewest possible assault operations and by conducting land campaigns only in decisive areas. The presently planned campaign, which involves to assaults followed by land campaigns in the Japanese homeland, is in conformity with this principle. [Further,* the extent of the objective area gives us an opportunity to effect surprise as to the points of landing and, once ashore, to profit by our superiority in mobility and mechanized power through maneuver. Should it be decided to follow the southern Kyushu operation by another operation such as against northern Kyushu in order to exploit bombardment and blockade, and should this bring about capitulation of the Japanese, the casualties should be less than for the presently planned campaign. We consider that at this time it would be a pure gamble that the Japanese would admit defeat under such conditions. If they do not, invasion of the Tokyo Plain might still be required with resultant increased total casualties.

The best estimate of casualties for these possible sequences of operations follows. For the reasons stated above, it is admittedly only an "educated guess".

	Killed In Action	Wounded in Action	Missing in Action	Total
Southern Kyushu, followed by Tokyo Plain, to mid-1946	40,000	150,000	3,500	193,500
Southern Kyushu - Northwestern Kyushu	25,000	105,000	2,500	132,500
Southern Kyushu - Northwestern Kyushu - Tokyo Plain	46,000	170,000	4,000	220,000

8. _Time._ Under the campaign as planned, it is estimated that the defeat of the Japanese in the Tokyo Plain area and the seizure of ports on Tokyo Bay would be completed by mid-1946. Should it prove necessary to execute other operations prior to invading the Tokyo Plain, the earliest date by which the latter operation could take place is estimated to be October 1946, because of adverse weather and ground conditions and the necessity of further mobilizing resources. In either case, the war should be over not later than the end of 1946. On the other hand, we are unable to estimate the time required or the losses that will result in an effo9rt to defeat Japan by isolation, blockade and bombardment without

invasion, because of our inability to predict at what stage thereof the Japanese might concede defeat, and because of the possibility that invasion of the Tokyo area would ultimate be necessary. E feel that at best, this strategy will lead to a long war, which would have an adverse effect upon the U.S. position vis-à-vis other nations who will, in the meantime, be rebuilding their peacetime economy.

9. In summary, our planned course of action is:

a. To proceed with an operation against southern Kyushu on 1 November 1945, as presently directed

b. To plan an invasion of the Tokyo area with a target date of 1 March 1946.

c. To exploit to the utmost in the interim periods the possibilities of blockade and air bombardment of Japan from positions in the Marianas, Iwo Jima, the Ryukyus and Kyushu.

d. To make preparations during the period following the assault on southern Kyushu for the invasion of the Tokyo area about 1 March 1946, or the extension of blockading positions to northwestern Kyusho on the same date.

e. To base the decision as to operations following southern Kyushu on developments.

10. Russian participation in the war. In previous discussions and correspondence with the Russians they have indicated generally their plan of campaign should they enter the war; that they would probably require about three months for concentration of troops and supplies on their east-

ern front; [that maintenance of the Pacific supply route would be necessary; and that it might be possible for the United States to base limited forces in Kamchatka and air forces in the Komsomolsk-Nikolaevsk area. In these discussions we were guided by the following basic principles:

Russia's entry at as early a date as possible consistent with her ability to engage in offensive operations is necessary to provide maximum assistance to our Pacific operations. The U.S. will provide maximum support possible without interfering with our main effort against Japan.

The objective of Russia's military effort against Japan in the Far East should be the defeat of the Japanese forces in Manchuria, air operations against Japan proper in collaboration with U.S. air forces based in eastern Siberia, and maximum interference with Japanese sea traffic between Japan and the mainland of Asia.

Nothing that has happened since is believed to require any change to these principles, except to note that we believe that we can defeat the Japanese in the main islands regardless of Russian entry, because of our own estimated ability to restrict movement of Japanese reinforcements from Asia. However, the defeat of the Japanese army in north China is still considered to be the best contribution that the Russians can make. We should insist that the appropriate U.S. command direct and control any Russian part in operations against Japanese sea traffic to Japan and in the air bombardment of Japan.

As to basing U.S. forces in Russian territory, this is no longer considered absolutely necessary, and we therefore propose to bring this subject up only if necessary in connection with Russian discussion of opening a sea route to other Pacific ports.

Opening a sea route to Russian ports may well be a resultant requirement of Russian entry into the war. We estimate that it might be satisfactorily accomplished by U.S. convoy of cargo ships in small groups without the necessity for our seizure of Japanese territory or of basing forces in Russian territory other than an advanced anchorage at Petropavlovsk and minor base facilities at the Russian termini. However, it should be noted that a more desirable plan would be to route the convoys through Tsushima Strait once it is under our control, thus avoiding the ice conditions of the northern straits. We should avoid by all possible means U.S. commitment to costly operations in the Kuriles-Karafuto area for this sole purpose.

In general, we believe that the best policy is not to press the Russians for further information or for any commitment, but merely to declare our readiness to receive and fully consider any proposals which they may wish to make.

11. Participation by other nations.

a. China. By the fall of 1945, the Chinese National Army will consist of about 2,500,000 men, of which only 36 divisions, now being trained under U.S. supervision, can be considered reasonably effective. There are approximately

500,000 unarmed recruits in training under the Chinese, and an estimated provincial and local militia totaling about 1,000,000. In addition, guerrillas under nominal control of the Central Government total about 300,000. The regular forces of the Chinese communist Armies amount to about 500,000.

b. British Empire forces.

Army: 1 Canadian, 1 New Zealand, and 3 Australian

Imperial Divisions will be deployed in the Pacific; approximately 23 divisions will be deployed in Southeast Asia, including English, Indian and African units.

Air Forces: Negotiations are in progress to make use of 10 squadrons of British bombers in the Pacific, with a possible ultimate employment of 20 squadrons. The RAF will provide the air units found necessary for operations in Southeast Asia.

Naval Forces: Elements of the British Fleet will support operations in Southeast Asia; 3 naval assault forces, comprising amphibious lift for about 3 divisions, will be available to the Southeast Asia Command. The British Pacific Fleet, consisting of 4 battleships, 5 carriers, accompanying light naval forces and train, is currently operating under Admiral Nimitz.

Estimated Japanese strength in Southeast Asia and Malaysia, excluding the Philippines, in the fall of 1945,is about 600,000 men. The British should be assigned the primary responsibility for the defeat of these forces. The British Pacific Fleet and elements of the RAF mentioned above will participate in the invasion of Japan.

c. France. Certain French naval vessels are now under operational control of the Southeast Asia Command. It does not appear practicable to support French naval vessels in Pacific operations. The French have offered a corps composed of two Colonial Divisions for operations in the Pacific. The question of where these divisions can be best employed is now being examined. The Southeast Asia Command includes minor French forces for clandestine operations in Indo-China.

d. Italy. From a military point of view Italian participation in the war against Japan is of negligible, if any, advantage to over-all conduct of the war.

e. Mexico. The 201^t Mexican Fighter Squadron is now operating in the Southwest Pacific area.

f. Portugal. If so desired by the Allies, Portugal stands ready to provide minor forces for occupation of Portuguese Timor.

g. The Netherlands. Dutch forces may fulfill a minor role in recapture of areas in the Netherlands East Indies.

We believe that offers from any nation of military and naval assistance in the Pacific war should be considered on their military merits, and should be accepted only in case the forces offered are trained and equipped to meet U.S. standards of combat efficiency, can be effectively employed in planned operations against Japan, are reasonably self-supporting, and operate under U.S. control.

12. In conclusion we desire to point out that throughout previous staff discussions with the

British we have emphasized that control and direction of the war against Japan lies with the U.S. We believe that we should continue to follow that policy and that efforts to bring the direction of the Pacific war under the laborious, argumentative and time-consuming system of combined control should be vigorously opposed.

Note: photostats "A," "B" and "C," following, appear to be missing from the files—Editor

TOP SECRET

TAB "A"

AIR COVERAGE AFTER DEVELOPMENT OF OKI-NAWA BASES
(One Phototat)

TOP SECRET

TAB "B"

AIR COVERAGE AFTER COMPLETION OF DEVEL-
OPMENT OF SOUTHERN KYUSHU BASES
(One Phototat)

TOP SECRET

TAB "C"

AIR COVERAGE AFTER COMPLETION OF DEVEL-
OPMENT OF TOKYO PLAIN BASES
(One Phototat)

TOP SECRET

TAB "D"

ESTIMATED JAPANESE DISPOSITIONS
1 NOVEMBER 1945
(One Phototat)

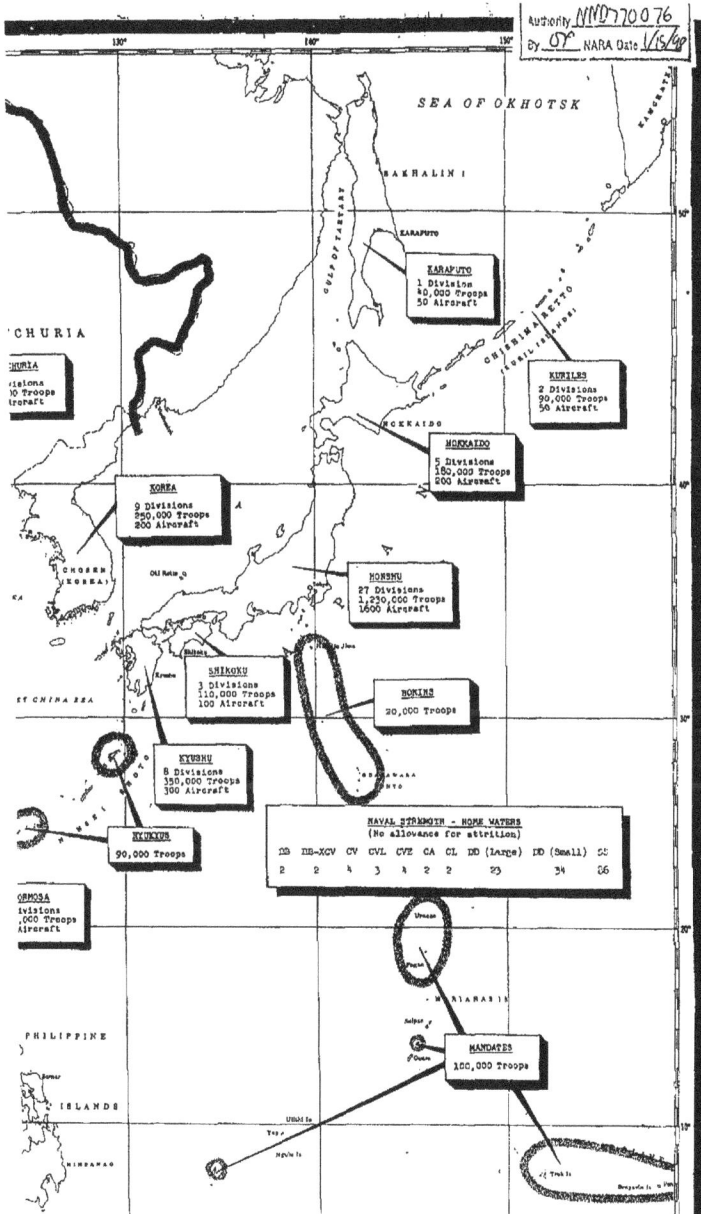

TOP SECRET

TAB "E"

GENERAL CONCEPT OF OPERATIONS
(One Phototat)

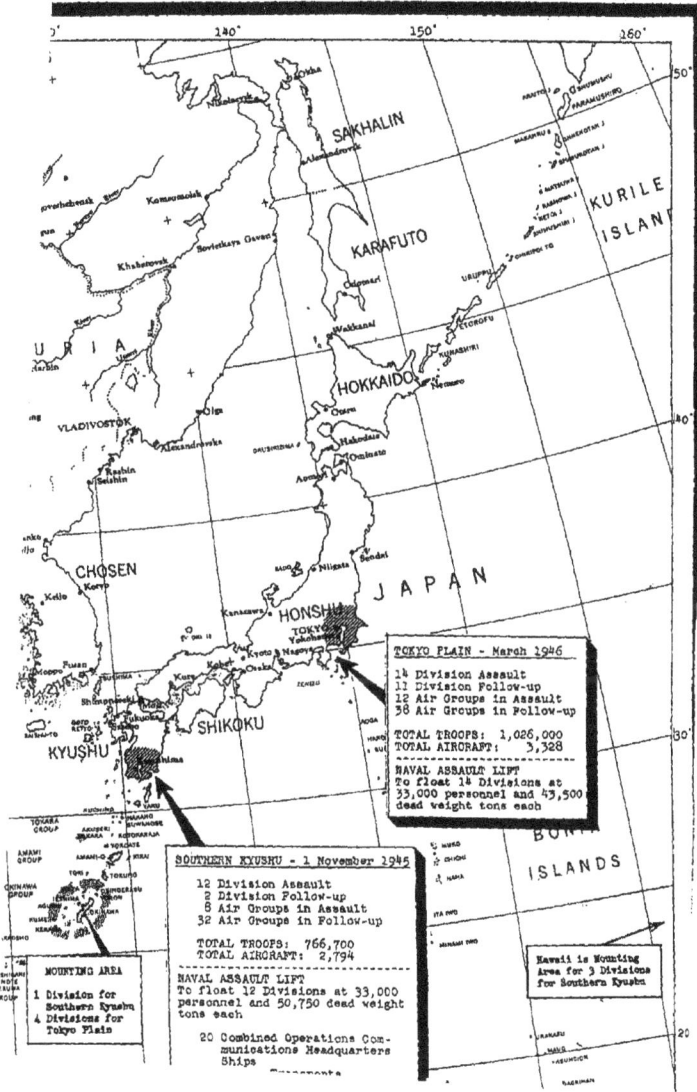

TAB "F"
SALIENT FACTS AND ESTIMATES
CAMPAIGNIN KOREA

1. Physiography and Climate. Rugged terrain in central and eastern parts with limited capital plains on west. Only feasible approach is via Yellow Sea to west coast. Changsan-got (90 miles SW of Heijo) is only suitable landing area for large force. Climate allows military operations throughout the year.

2. Enemy strength and capabilities.

a. Air. About 5000 planes of all types. Present Japanese policy of employing suicide tactics permits use of all types of planes. Doubtful if effort in Korea would ever exceed 200 sorties per day. This would fall off rapidly since all out effort not expected.

b. Naval. Submarines and suicide craft would be employed in large numbers but use of heavy units not probable.

c. Ground. In Korea 6 divisions of fresh troops. These could quickly concentrate in objective area since only one feasible landing area exists. 25 divisions in Manchuria. Their use depends on Russia.

3. Strategic considerations.

a. Advantages.

(1) Occupation of even a limited area would go far towards completing the isolation of Japan.

(2) A beachhead area capable of basing 800-1000 planes could be seized and held.

(3) Aircraft could operate effectively against enemy lines of communication in North China,

Manchuria, Korea and the Yellow Sea and assist in strategic bombing of Japan.

b. Disadvantages.

(1) Requires a large scale amphibious assault without benefit of land-based air against a region virtually unaffected by the war.

(2) Would risk involvement with Kwantung and North China armies in a position relatively difficult for us to reinforce.

(3) It would require the employment of 12-15 divisions in active defense of even a limited beachhead and a logistic strain for the support of such a force which would affect our capabilities for subsequent action.

4. Conclusion. The results to be obtained by an attack on Korea are not commensurate with the costs.

TAB "G"
SALIENT FACTS AND ESTIMATES
CAMPAIGN IN NORTHWSTERN KYUSHU
As an Operation Following Okinawa

1. Physiography. Terrain is suitable for establishment of a base of operations for:
a. Air and naval blockade of Yellow Sea, Tsushima Strait, and Sea of Japan.
b. Opening a sea route to Russian ports.
c. Destroying enemy forces in northern Kyushu.
2. Initial Objective. Fukuoka Area.
3. Enemy Forces.
a. 3 divisions and 2 depot divisions in northern Kyushu.
b. 3 divisions in southern Kyushu.
c. 125,000 lightly armed and partly trained reservists.
d. Reinforcements—possibly 6 divisions.
e. Maximum air effort—400 to 500 sorties in any 24-hour period.
f. Naval forces chiefly submarines, midget submarines, and small suicide surface craft.
Enemy will make desperate effort to defend this area.
4. Own Forces Required.
a. 17 infancy divisions, 1 armored division, 2 airborne divisions.
b. Air forces—37 groups or 2,600 aircraft.
c. Naval forces.
(1) 155 major combatant units.
(2) 426 light combatant units.
(3) 255 light vessels for minesweeping, etc.

(4) Simultaneous transport lift for 12 divisions (180 APAs, 72 AKAs, plus smaller types). Forces to be landed in first 30 days—365,000. Total forces to be landed—850,000.

5. Discussion. In the restricted waters of this area, carrier-borne aircraft cannot meet requirements of an operation of this size. There must be land-based fighters within 300 miles. Okinawa is 520 miles from Fukuoka.

6. Conclusion. Northwestern Kyushu is not suitable as an invasion objective until land-based fighters are established within 300 miles.

DOCUMENT 6
16 June 1945   COPY NO. 48
Pages 1-19, incl.   (SPECIAL DISTRIBUTION)

JOINT CHIEFS OF STAFF
DETAILS OF THE CAMPAIGN AGAINST JAPAN
Report by the Joint Staff Planners

The Joint Staff Planners recommend that the
enclosure be presented to the President.

DITRIBUTION	COPY NO.
Admiral Leahy	1
General Marshall	2 & 5
Admiral King	3 & 6
General Arnold	4
General Handy	7
Admiral Edwards	8
Admiral Cooke	9
General Hull	10
General Norstad	11
Admiral Duncan	12
General Cabalt	13
General Lincoln	14

ENCLOSURE

MEMORANDUM FOR THE PRESIDENT:
Subject: Campaign against Japan.

1. Strategy. Throughout the series of staff conferences with the British, we have agreed that the over-all concept for the prosecution of the war included provision "to bring about at the earliest possible date the unconditional surrender of Japan." We believe that the only sure way, and certainly the quickest way to force the surrender of Japan is to defeat her armed forces in the main Japanese islands. Hence, at recent staff conferences we have proposed—and the British have agreed—that the over-all objective of the Japanese war is "to force the unconditional surrender of Japan by (1) lowering Japanese ability and will to resist by establishing sea and air blockades, conducting intensive air bombardment and destroying Japanese air and naval strength; (2) invading and seizing objectives in the industrial heart of Japan."

It is by no means certain that a capitulation by a Japanese government will be recognized by Japanese armed forces everywhere. If, following such an acknowledgement, here forces do not surrender, their position will be so seriously weakened as to facilitate their defeat in detail. However, the possibility must be faced that the Japanese forces everywhere must be defeated.

2. Presently planned campaign. Our agreed conception of operations for the main effort in the Pacific war is:

"Following the Okinawa operation to seize additional positions to intensify the blockade and air bombardment of Japan in order to create a situation favorable to:

"An assault on Kyushu for the purpose of further reducing Japanese capabilities by containing and destroying major enemy forces and further intensifying the blockade and air bombardment in order to establish a tactical condition favorable to:

"The decisive invasion of the industrial heart of Japan through the Tokyo Plain."

Our campaign plans have therefore been designed to seize positions progressively closer to the Tokyo Plain—the political, industrial and communication center of Japan—with a view to isolating the Japanese islands and providing sufficient bases from which, by sea and air bombardment, conditions will be created which will make ultimate invasion of the Tokyo Plain acceptable and feasible. We have also endeavored so to design the campaign that the Japanese cannot fail to see and feel the results of its rapidly increasing tempo and magnitude, with the thought that at some stage of the campaign they will admit defeat in order to avoid further destruction.

Thus far in this campaign we have seized and developed air and naval bases in the Marianas, Iwo Jima, the Philippines and Okinawa. No further operations in the Ryukyus after completion of the Okinawa campaign are now contemplated; all available resources are being utilized to develop air and naval bases in Okinawa to maximum capacity by November 1945. By then it is expected to have about 2700 land-based aircraft operating from this area and to have completed an advanced fleet base and anchorage. The map, Tab "A", shows the land-based aircraft expected to be based within range of Japan by that time and the areas they can reach. Meanwhile every effort is also being made to transport to the Pacific from Europe the added means required for a rapid and decisive campaign. In general the units needed to build the required bases are being moved first, followed by the required additional combat units, air and ground.

Already we have eliminated practically all Japanese sea traffic between their main islands and points to the southward of Shanghai, and severely restricted their traffic to Shanghai and Yellow Sea ports. By November 1945, when air operations from Okinawa will be in full swing, there should remain to the Japanese only those sea routes across Tsushima Strait to Korea and across the Sea of Japan. It should be noted that our air and submarines are already operating in these areas on a limited scale. By November 1945 the Japanese situation is expected to be critical. Their fleet units in home waters have already been so reduced s to no longer constitute a controlling strategic factor. Their air arm is already committing training planes to combat and will probably continue to devote much of their remaining air power to suicide tactics. Their ability to move ground forces to Japan from Asia or vice versa is already reduced and is estimated by 1 November to be not more than one division a month. The map, Tab "D", shows the estimated

Japanese dispositions of ground and air forces about 1 November 1945.

In order to obtain bases still closer to the Tokyo Plain from which to augment sea and air bombardment, complete the isolation of the main Japanese islands and to provide land based air cover and support for the invasion of the Tokyo Plain, should that prove necessary, we have directed General MacArthur and Admiral Nimitz to invade southern Kyushu about 1 November 1945.

We have not yet directed the execution of any operations after the invasion of southern Kyushu, feeling that decision would better await further developments. However, plans and preparations are being made to invade the Tokyo Plain—the political, industrial and communication center of Japan—about 4 months after the southern Kyushu operation, or about 1 March 1946. We consider that this operation should be decisive. By planning and preparing for a supreme operation of this magnitude, we shall be in a position to undertake any lesser operation should developments warrant.

In the period prior to the planned invasion of the Tokyo Plain, every effort will be made to exploit the blockade and bombardment of Japan. In this period, from bases presently and prospectively available, more bombs will be dropped on Japan than were delivered against Germany during the entire European war. If this blockade and bombardment achieve decisive results, these will, in all probability, be brought about by this scale of effort prior to the planned date for the invasion of the Tokyo Plain. However, in the event this invasion is not considered feasible and acceptable on the planned date, a course of action to extend bombardment and blockade is open to us.

3. Examination of the map, Tab "A", shows that bases on the Asiatic mainland other than in Korea are too distant to be of value in augmenting our present capabilities for sea and air bombardment of Japan and in cutting the remaining Japanese sea routes across Tsushima Strait and the Sea of Japan. Furthermore, the blockade of the Yellow Sea and the sea areas to the southward is now virtually effective. There is also the likelihood that any operation in North China, with its vast area and large numbers of Japanese ground forces, will develop into a vacuum drawing even more and more U.S. forces into an indecisive and costly campaign. We therefore discarded, as unnecessary and diversionary, operations to seize bases on the coast of North China. The best areas from which to complete the isolation of Japan are obviously either in Korea or in the southwestern part of the Japanese Archipelago. We considered three possibilities: Korea, the northwestern part of Kyushu, and southern Kyushu. Tab "F" shows the salient facts and estimates for campaigns in Korea.

We discarded Korea as a possible operation to follow Okinawa because of its longer sea approach, the paucity of good beaches and exits therefrom, the rugged terrain back of the beaches, the few airfield sites available for development after seizure, and the great reinforcement capabilities of the Japanese from their fine and as yet untouched army in northern China. Furthermore, because of the distance from Okinawa bases, we would have great difficulty in interfering by air action with the arrival of Japanese reinforcements and in providing adequate air cover and support to the assault. The campaign is estimated to require about the same commitment of forces as for the invasion of southern Kyushu (14 divisions).

Similarly we considered northwestern Kyushu unsuitable as an initial objective are following Okinawa because the sea approaches to the best landing area are restricted, well fortified and heavily mined; and because of Japanese capability to reinforce the area from two directions—from southern Kyushu and from Honshu. The forces required for such an operation are estimated to be in excess of those for southern Kyushu.

The seizure of southern Kyushu has been directed because:

a. Its occupation is essential both for decisive assault on the Tokyo Plain and strangulation of Japan through bombardment and through isolation from Korea and the mainland of Asia;

b. It is the most logical extension of our operations in the Ryukyus, since shore-based tactical air support can be furnished from Okinawa and lines of communication are shorter than for any other practicable objective;

c. Airfields on which to base approximately 40 groups (over 2500 aircraft) can be developed, from which we can practically sever Japan's last remaining communication with the mainland of Asia and from which the air bombardment of the remainder of Japan can be greatly intensified;

d. It will contribute toward the defeat of Japanese armies in the Japanese homeland;

e. It may well be that Japanese capitulation will be forced by this operation.

4. As to other areas, Admiral Mountbatten in the Southeast Asian Command plans to seize a position in the Port Swettenham-Port Dixon areas on the Malay Peninsula in the latter half of August 1945 and to follow this up with a campaign to recapture Singapore beginning probably in December-January. General Wedemeyer has advised that, in China, the Generalissimo. To launch an overland advance with Chinese forces on the canton-Hong Kong area beginning about 1 September 1945 and to follow up any Japanese withdrawals northward along the railroad route in central China.

5. Plans for the period after the invasion of the Tokyo Plain cannot be made with firmness at this time. If the Japanese continue to resist, plans must provide for further operations in the main islands and for operations by ourselves or our allies on the mainland of Asia against those Japanese forces which continue to resist. We are striving to keep U.S. commitments on the mainland to a minimum, through encouraging and supporting maximum effort by the Chinese, and by the Russians if they should enter the war. Hence, plans provide for continued U.S. aid to Chinese forces, the scale of which can probably be materially increased later in the campaign.

Should the Japanese unconditionally surrender or concede defeat during the campaign in Japan proper, there will still remain the sizable task of disarming their forces everywhere, assembling them at ports, and returning them to their home islands.

6. Forces required for presently planned campaign. Estimates of the forces required to execute the invasion of southern Kyushu and of the Tokyo Plain are shown on the map, Tab "E". The maps, Tabs "B" and "C", show the deployment of land-based aircraft planned upon the completion of each of these two operations. It is obvious from the maps that this air power will cover Japan and the approaches thereto with a blanket of destruction.

For the campaign as planned through the invasion of the Tokyo Plain, it is expected there will be in the Pacific theaters, India-Burma and China, by the spring of 1946 a total of 39 Army divisions and 127 Army air groups (8,500 land-based aircraft) or a grand total in Army forces of about 3,000,000 men. General MacArthur has indicated that if operations are necessary after the invasion of the Tokyo Plain, plans should begin for the movement of additional divisions from the U.S. to the Pacific at a rate of about 4 additional divisions per month, from a planned strategic reserve of 17 divisions in the U.S.

By 1 March 1946 the following number of major combat ships are scheduled to be fully operational in the Pacific Fleet:

10 BB (Battleships)
13 OBB (Old Battleships)
2 CB (Large Cruisers)
22 CV (Aircraft Carriers)
2 CVB (Aircraft Carriers (Large))
9 CVL (Aircraft Carriers (Small))
74 CVE (43 combat)
Aircraft Carriers, Escort)
26 CA (Heavy Cruisers)
33 CL (Light Cruisers)
8 CL (AA) (Light Cruisers) (Antiaircraft)
364 DD (Destroyers)
326 DE (Destroyer Escort Vessels)
189 Ss (Submarines)

The above figures make no allowance for attrition. Three months after the Kyushu operation it is estimated that approximately 10% will either have been lost or still undergoing repairs to damage received in this operation. Of the operational ships in service 75% will normally be constantly available for any single operation. Others will be either undergoing operational repairs or be otherwise employed.

It is estimated that approximately 3,600 carrier-based aircraft will be available on 1 march 1946.

As a general statement it may be said that the forces of all arms which are required for the operations we contemplate are all those which can be effectively employed and supported in the theater within the means which will be available to us. We feel that the unremitting application of this maximum forces is essential to defeating

Japan at the least possible cost in lives and resources.

7. Casualties. The cost in casualties of the main operations against Japan are not subject to accurate estimate. The scale of Japanese resistance in the past has not been (predictable?). Casualty expectancy rates based on experience in the Pacific vary greatly from the short bloody battle of Tarawa to the unopposed landing at Linguyen. It would be difficult to predict whether operations on Kyushu would more closely resemble the fighting on Okinawa or whether it would parallel the battle of Leyte. However, it may be pointed out that the extent of the objective areas in both Kyushu and Honshu gives us an opportunity to effect surprise as to the points of landing and, once ashore, to profit by our superiority in mobility and mechanized power through maneuver.

Certain general conclusions can, be reached. The highest casualty rate occurs during the assault phase of an amphibious operation; casualties in land warfare are a function of the length of campaign and of the scale of opposition encountered. Naval casualties can be expected to vary directly with the number of amphibious operations involved and with the length of the campaign. Casualties can be kept to a minimum, then, by terminating the war at the earliest possible time by means of the fewest possible assault operations and by conducting land campaigns only in decisive areas. The presently planned campaign, which involves two assaults followed by land campaigns in the Japanese homeland, is in conformity with this principle.

8. Time. Under the campaign as planned, it is estimated that the defeat of the Japanese in the Tokyo Plain area and the seizure of ports on Tokyo Bay would be completed by mid-1946. Should it prove necessary to execute other operations prior to invading the Tokyo Plain, the earliest date by which the latter operation could take place is estimated to be October 1946, because of adverse weather and ground conditions and the necessity of further mobilizing resources. In either case, the war should be over not later than the end of 1946.

On the other hand, we are unable to estimate the time required or the losses that will result in an effort to defend Japan by isolation, blockade and bombardment without invasion, because of our inability to predict at what stage thereof the Japanese might concede defeat, and because of the possibility that invasion of the Tokyo area would ultimately be necessary. We feel that at best, such strategy would lead to a longer and probably more costly war.

9. In summary, our planned course of action is:

a. To proceed with an operation against southern Kyushu on 1 November 1945, as presently directed.

b. To plan and prepare for an invasion of the Tokyo area with a target date of 1 March 1946.

c. To exploit to the utmost in the interim periods the possibilities of blockade and air bombardment of Japan from positions in the Marianas, Iwo Jima, the Ryukyus and Kyushu.

d. To base the decision as to operations following southern Kyushu on developments.

10. Russian participation in the war. In previous discussions and correspondence with the Russians they have indicated that they would probably require about three months after VE-Day for concentration of troops and supplies on their eastern front. We have considered that Russia's entry at as early a date as possible consistent with her ?? to engage in offensive operations is highly desirable to provide maximum assistance to our Pacific operations and that the primary objective of Russia's military effort should be to contain and destroy Japanese forces in Manchuria.

We believe that we can defeat the Japanese in the main islands regardless of Russian entry, because of our own estimated ability to restrict movement of Japanese reinforcements from Asia. However, the defeat of the Japanese army in North China including Manchuria would be a valuable contribution to the early and economical termination of the war.

As to basing U.S. forces in Russian territory, this is no longer considered necessary, and we therefore suggest that this subject be discussed only if necessary in connection with Russian discussion of opening a sea route to their Pacific ports.

Opening a sea route to Russian ports may well be a resultant requirement of Russian entry into the war. We estimate that it might be satisfactorily accomplished by U.S. convoy of cargo ships in small groups without the necessity for our seizure of Japanese territory or of basing forces in Russian territory other than an advanced anchorage at Petropavlovsk and minor base facilities at the Russian termini. However, it should be noted that a more desirable plan would be to route the convoys through Tsushina Strait once it is under our control, thus avoiding the ice conditions of the Northern straits. We should avoid by all possible means U.S. commitment to costly operations in the Kuriles-Karafuto area for this solo purpose.

In general, we believe that the best policy is not to present the Russians for further information or for any commitment, but merely to declare our readiness to receive and fully consider any proposals which they may wish to make.

11. Participation by other nations.

a. China. By the fall of 1945, the Chinese National Army will consist of about 2,500,000 men, of which only 36 divisions, now being trained under U.S. supervision, can be considered reasonably effective. There are approximately 500,000 unarmed recruits in training under the Chinese, and an estimated provincial and local militia totaling about 1,000,000. In addition, guerrillas under nominal control of the Central Government total about 300,000. The regular forces of the Chinese Communist Armies amount to about 500,000.

It is estimated that Japanese strength in China in the fall of 1945 excluding Manchuria, will be about 900,000 men. Therefore, it is considered that the major share of that task of defeating the enemy in China south of Manchuria should fall to China.

b. British Empire forces.

Army: 1 Canadian, 1 New Zealand, and 3 Australian Imperial Divisions will be deployed in the Pacific; approximately 23 divisions will be deployed in Southeast Asia, including English, Indian and African units.

Air Forces: Negotiations are in progress to make use of 10 squadrons of British bombers in the Pacific, with a possible ultimate employment of 20 squadrons. The RAF will provide the air units found necessary for operations in Southeast Asia.

Naval Forces: Elements of the British Fleet will support operations in Southeast Asia; 3 naval assault forces, comprising amphibious lift for about 3 divisions, will be available to the Southeast Asia Command. The British Pacific Fleet, consisting of 4 battleships, 5 carriers, accompanying light naval forces and train, is currently operating under Admiral Nimitz.

Estimated Japanese strength in Southeast Asia and Malaysia, excluding the Philippines, in the fall of 1945, is about 600,000 men. The British should continue their primary responsibility for the mop-up of those forces. The British Pacific Fleet and elements of the RAF mentioned above will participate in the invasion of Japan.

c. France. Certain French naval vessels are now under operational control of the British East Indies Fleet. It does not appear practicable or desirable to employ French naval vessels or air forces in Pacific operations. The French have offered a corps composed of two Colonial divisions for operations in the Pacific. The question of where and when these divisions can be best employed is now being examined. Arrangements for the French must include adequate provisions against any repetition in the Pacific of the French refusals, which have occurred in Europe, to obey military orders. The Southeast Asia Command includes minor French forces for clandestine operations in Indo-China.

d. Portugal. If so desired by the allies, Portugal stands ready to provide minor forces for occupation of Portuguese Timor.

e. The Netherlands. Dutch forces may fulfill a minor role in recapture of areas in the Netherlands East Indies.

We believe that offers from any nation to contribute token or minor assistance in the Pacific war should be considered on their military merits. The acceptance of any forces should be the bases that they are to be trained and equipped to met U.S. standards of combat efficiency, can be effectively employed in planned operations against Japan, are reasonably self-supporting, and will operate as determined by the U.S.

12. Control and Command in the Pacific War.

Throughout previous staff discussions with the British we have taken the position that control, command and direction of the war in the Pacific lies with the U.S. The British thus far have committed their forces under this arrangement and have followed U.s. lead and policy. We believe that we should continue to follow that policy and that any efforts which may be made to bring the direction of the Pacific war under the laborious, argumentative and time-consuming system of combined control should be vigorously opposed.

TOP SECRET

ENCLOSURE
PROPOSED REVISION OF J.C.S. 1388
"DETAILS OF THE CAMPAIGN AGAINST JAPAN:

Replace last 4 subparagraphs of paragraph 6, page 7 with the following. (Additions underscored, deletions lined out).

~~By 1 March 1946 the following number of major combat ships are scheduled to be fully operational in the Pacific Fleet.~~ By 1 March 1946 the following major naval vessels are scheduled for deployment in the Pacific:
10 BB (Battleships)
13 OBB (Old Battleships)
2 CB (Large Cruisers)
22 CV (Aircraft Carriers)
2 CVB (Aircraft Carriers (Large))
9 CVL (Aircraft Carriers (Small))
74 CVE (43 combat)
(Aircraft Carriers, Escort)
17 AGC (Operations and Command (Headquarters Ships)
223 APA (Attack Transport Ships)
108 AKA (Attack Cargo Ships)
26 CA (Heavy Cruisers)
33 CL (Light Cruisers)
8 CL (AA) (Light Cruisers)
(Antiaircraft)
364 DD (Destroyers)
326 DE (Destroyer Escort Vessels)
189 SS (Submarines)

799 LST (Tank Landing Ships)
491 LSM (Medium Landing Ships)

The above figures make no allowance for attrition. Three months after the Kyushu operation it is estimated that approximately 10% will either have been lost or still undergoing repairs to damage received in this operation. Of the operational ships in service 75% will ~~normally~~ be constantly available for any single operation. Others will be either undergoing operational repairs or be otherwise employed. <u>It is worthy of note that the amphibious resources listed above will permit simultaneous assault landings on a scale never before thought possible.</u>

It is estimated that approximately 3,600 carrier-based aircraft will be available on 1 March 1946.

As a general statement it may be said that the forces of all arms which are required <u>and which should be employed</u> for the operations we contemplate are all those which can be ~~effectively employed and~~ supported in the theater within the means which will be available to us <u>and which can be effectively employed</u>. We feel that the unremitting application of this maximum force is essential to defeating Japan at the least possible cost in lives and resources.

<u>Replace Paragraph 7, Pages 7 and 8, with following paragraph.</u>
7. <u>Casualties.</u> Our casualty experience in the Pacific war has been so diverse as to throw serious doubt on the validity of any quantitative esti-

mate of casualties for future operations. The following data indicate results of experience.

Campaign	U.S. Casualties Killed, wounded, missing	Jap Casualties Killed and Prisoners (Not including wounded)	Ratio U.S. to Jap
Leyte	17,000	78,000	1:4.6
Luzon	31,000	156,000	1:5.0
Iwo Jima	20,000	25,000	1:1.25
Okinawa	34,000 (Ground	81,000	1:2
	7,700 (Navy)	(not a complete count)	
Normandy (1st 30 days)	42,000	—	—

The record of General MacArthur's operations from 1 March 1944 through 1 May 1945 shows 13,742 U.S. killed compared to 310,165 Japanese killed, or a ratio of 22 to 1.

The nature of the objective area in Kyushu gives maneuver room for land and sea operations. For these and other resources it is probable that the cost in ground force casualties for the first 30 days of the Kyushu operation will be on the order of that for Luzon. Naval casualties will probably be at about the divisions) are being trained under U.S. supervision and can be considered reasonably effective for offensive operations. Some of the balance of the Chinese Armies are capable of defensive or occupation operations while the large remainder, for logistical, political and other reasons, are ineffective. Increase of supply to the Chinese Armies is dependent on the opening of a sea route to a major China coast port. Though we are planning to send several ship loads of supplies to General Wedemeyer this summer, contingent upon his seizing a harbor, no substantial diversion of ships and men for this purpose can be made until the campaign in Japan

93

will permit.

It is estimated that Japanese strength in China in the fall of 1945 excluding Manchuria, will be about 900,000 men. Therefore, it is considered that the major share of the task of defeating the enemy in China south of Manchuria should fall to China.

Replace paragraph 11 b, page 11
with the following paragraph.

b. British Empire (Commonwealth) Forces.

Army: 1 Canadian division has been accepted for participation in CORONET. 3 Australian Imperial divisions are currently being employed in Southwest Pacific Area under U.S. command. He British Chiefs of Staff have proposed (C.C.S. 889) a further contribution of 3-5 British Commonwealth Divisions to participate in the final phase of the campaign in Japan, all to operate under U.S. command. The views of the Australian and New Zealand Governments on this proposal have been requested by the British Chiefs of Staff, but not yet received. The British intend deploying Commonwealth forces to the extent of 21 divisions and 16 brigades (probably including the above 3-5 divisions) in the Southeast Asia-East Indies area. Under separate consideration is acceptance by the U.S. of 1 Australian division to participate in operations against Japan proper; acceptance of the British offer in C.C.S. 889 will probably eliminate this offer.

Air Forces: Negotiations are in progress to make use of 10 squadrons of British bombers in the Pacific, with a possible ultimate employment of 20 squadrons. Also a force of approximately 15 tactical squadrons have been offered for support of the 3-5 divisions indicated above. The RAF will provide air units found necessary for operations in Southeast Asia.

Naval Forces: Elements of the British Fleet will support operations in Southeast Asia; 3 naval assault forces, comprising amphibious lift for about 3 divisions, will be continuously available to the southeast Asia Command, should these elements not be used in the main operations against Japan. The British Pacific Fleet, consisting of 4 battleships, 5 carriers, accompanying light naval forces and train, is currently operating under Admiral Nimitz. In addition, elements of the East Indies Fleet are offered for support of the 3-5 divisions proposed above.

Estimated Japanese strength in Southeast Asia and Malaysia, excluding the Philippines, in the fall of 1945, is about 600,000 men. The British should continue their primary responsibility for mopping-up the Japanese in SEA and the East Indies, exclusive of the Philippines. Acceptance of the latest proposed British Commonwealth contributions to the final phase of the war against Japan (C.C.S. 889) should not prejudice early accomplishment of this task provided the assault lift available to SACSEA is not employed elsewhere. The British Pacific Fleet, elements of the Royal Air Force, one Canadian division and possibly the Commonwealth force proposed in C.C.S. 889 will participate in the operation for invasion of Japan. It is the intention of the Joint Chiefs of Staff to turn over to British command certain portions of the SWPAC area including Australia, the Solomons, New Guinea, New Britain, New Ireland and the Netherlands East Indies.

DOCUMENT 7

MEMORANDUM FOR THE CHIEF OF STAFF
SUBJECT: Amplifying Comments on Planners'
Paper for Presentation to the President.

The following points are arranged seriatim in
accordance with the appearance of the same sub-
jects in the paper the Planners propose for presentation to the President:

1. Our air and sea power has already greatly
reduced movement of Jap shipping south of
Korea and should in the next few months out of
it to a trickle if not choke it off entirely. Hence,
there is no need for seizing further positions in
order to block Japanese communications south of
Korea.

2. General MacArthur and Admiral Nimitz are
in agreement with the Chiefs of Staff in selecting
1 November as the target date to go into Kyushu
because by that time:

a. If we press preparations we can be ready.

b. Our estimates are that our air action will
have smashed practically every industrial target

worth hitting in Japan as well as destroying huge areas in the Jap cities.

c. The Japanese Navy, if any still exists, will be completely powerless.

d. Our sea action and air power will have cut Jap reinforcement capabilities from the mainland to negligible proportions.

Important considerations bearing on the 1 November date rather than a later one are the weather and cutting to a minimum Jap time for preparation of defenses. If we delay much after the beginning of November the weather situation in the succeeding months may be such that the invasion of Japan, and hence the end of the war, will be delayed for up to 6 months.

3. An outstanding military point about attacking Korea is the difficult terrain and beach conditions which appear to make the only acceptable assault areas Fusan in the southeast corner and Keijo, well up the western side. To get to Fusan, which is a strongly fortified area, we must move large and vulnerable assault forces past heavily fortified Japanese ?????? operation appears more difficult and costly than assault on Kyushu. Keijo appears an equally difficult and costly operation. After we have undertaken either one of them we still will not be as far forward as going into Kyushu.

4. The Kyushu operation is essential to a strategy of strangulation and appears to be the least costly worth-while operation following Okinawa. The basic point is that a lodgement in Kyushu is essential, both to tightening our strangle hold of blockade and bombardment on Japan,

and to forcing capitulation by invasion of the Tokyo Plain.

5. We are bringing to bear against the Japanese every weapon and all the force we can employ and there is no reduction in our maximum possible application of bombardment and blockade, while at the same time we are pressing invasion preparations. It seems that if the Japanese are ever willing to capitulate short of complete military defeat in the field they will do it when faced by the completely hopeless prospect occasioned by (1) destruction already wrought by air bombardment and sea blockade, coupled with (2) a landing on Japan indicating the firmness of our resolution, and also perhaps coupled with (3) the entry or threat of entry of Russia into the war.

6. With reference to clean-up of the Asiatic mainland, our objective should be to get the Russians to deal with the Japs in Manchuria (and Korea if necessary) and to vitalize the Chinese to a point where, with assistance of American air power and some supplies, they can map out their own country.

7. Casualties. Our experience in the pacific war is so diverse as to casualties that it is considered wrong to give any estimate in numbers. Using various combinations of Pacific experience, the War Department staff reaches the conclusion that the cost of securing a worth-while position in Korea would almost certainly be greater than the cost of the Kyushu operation. Points on the optimistic side of the Kyushu operation are that: General MacArthur has not yet accepted respon-

sibility for going ashore where there would be disproportionate casualties. The nature of the objective area gives room for maneuver, both on the land and by sea. As to any discussion of specific operations, the following data is pertinent:

Campaign	U.S. Casualties Killed, wounded, missing	Jap Casualties Killed and Prisoners (Not including wounded)	Ratio U.S. to Jap
Leyte	17,000	78,000	1:4.6
Luzon	31,000	156,000	1:5.0
Iwo Jima	20,000	25,000	1:1.25
Okinawa	34,000 (Ground	81,000	1:2
	7,700 (Navy)	(not a complete count)	
Normandy (1st 30 days)	42,000	—	—

The record of General MacArthur's operations from 1 March 1944 through 1 May 1945 shows 13,742 U.S. killed compared to 310,165 Japanese killed, or a ratio of 22 to 1.

There is reason to believe that the first 30 days in Kyushu should not exceed the price we have paid for Luzon. It is a grim fact that there is not an easy, bloodless way to victory in war and it is the thankless task of the leaders to maintain their firm outward front which holds the resolution of their subordinates. Any irresolution in the leaders may result in costly weakening and indecision in the subordinates. It was this basic difficulty with the Prime Minister which clouded and hampered all our preparations for the cross-channel operation now demonstrated as having been essential to victory in Europe.

8. An important point about Russian participation in the war is that the impact of Russian entry on the already hopeless Japanese may well

be the decisive action lowering them into capitulation at that time or shortly thereafter if we land in Japan.

9. In considering the matte of command and control in the Pacific war which the British wish to raise at the next conference, we must bear in mind the point that anything smacking of combined command in the Pacific might increase the difficulties with Russia and perhaps with China. Furthermore the obvious inefficiencies of combined command may directly result in increased cost in resources and American lives.

J.E.H.

Lt. Gen. John E. Hall

Document 8

BASIC MILITARY OBJECTIVES, STRATEGY, AND
POLICIES IN THE WAR AGAINST JAPAN
NO. 598

J.C.S. Files
*Memorandum by the Secretary of the Joint
Chiefs of Staff (McFarland)*

TOP SECRET

MINUTES OF MEETING HELD AT THE WHITE
HOUSE ON MONDAY, 18 JUNE 1945 AT 1530[1]

Present[:]   The President
        Fleet Admiral William D. Leahy
        General of the Army G. C. Marshall
        Fleet Admiral E. J. King
        Lieut. General I. C. Eaker (Representing
General of the Army H. H. Arnold)
        The Secretary of War, Mr. Stimson
        The Secretary of the Navy, Mr. Forrestal
        The Assistant Secretary of War, Mr. McCloy

Secretary
Brig. General A. J. McFarland

1. DETAILS OF THE CAMPAIGN AGAINST JAPAN

The President stated that he had called the meeting for the purposes of informing himself with no respect to the details of the campaign against Japan set out in Admiral Leahy's memorandum to the Joint Chiefs of Staff of 14 June[2]. He asked General Marshall if he would express his opinion. General Marshall pointed out that the present situation with respect to operations against Japan was practically identical with the situation which had existed in connection with the operations proposed against Normandy. He then read, as an expression of his views, the following digest of a memorandum prepared by the Joint chiefs of Staff for presentation to the President (J. C. S. 1388):[3]

Our air and sea power has already greatly reduced movement of Jap shipping south of Korea and should in the next few months cut it to a trickle if not choke it off entirely. Hence, there is no need for seizing further positions in order to block Japanese communications south of Korea.

General MacArthur and Admiral Nimitz are in agreement with the Chiefs of Staff in selecting 1 November as the target date to get into Kyushu because by that time:

a. If we press preparations we can be ready.

b. Our estimates are that our air action will have smashed practically every industrial target worth hitting in Japan as well as destroying huge areas in the Jap cities.

c. The Japanese Navy, if any still exists, will be completely powerless.

d. Our sea actin and air power will have cut Jap reinforcement capabilities from the mainland to negligible proportions.

Important considerations bearing on the 1 November date rather than a later one are the weather and cutting to a minimum Jap time for preparation of defenses. If we delay much after the beginning of November the weather situation in the succeeding months may be such that the invasion of Japan, and hence the end of the war, will be delayed for up to 6 months.

An outstanding military point about attacking Korea is the difficult terrain and beach conditions which appear to make the only acceptable assault areas Fusan [*Pusan*] in the southeast corner and Keijo [*Seoul*], well up the western side. To get to Fusan, which is a strongly fortified area, we must move large and vulnerable assault forces past heavily fortified Japanese areas. The operation appears more difficult and costly than assault on Kyushu. Keijo appears an equally difficult and costly operation. After we have undertaken either one of them we still will not be as far forward as going into Kyushu.

The Kyushu operation is essential to a strategy of strangulation and appears to be the least costly worthwhile operation following Okinawa. The basic point is that a lodgement in Kyushu is essential both to tightening our strangle hold of blockade and bombardment on Japan, and to forcing capitulation by invasion of the Tokyo Plain.

We are bringing to bear against the Japanese every weapon and all the force we can employ and there is no reduction in our maximum possible application of bombardment and blockade, while at the same time we are pressing invasion preparations. It seems that if Japanese are ever willing to capitulate short of complete military defeat in the field they will do it when faced by the completely hopeless prospect occasioned by (1) destruction already wrought by bombardment and sea blockade, coupled with (2) a landing on Jap indicating the firmness of our resolution, and also perhaps coupled with (3) the entry or threat of entry of Russia into the war.

With reference to clean-up of the Asiatic mainland, our objective should be to get the Russians to deal with the Japs in Manchuria (and Korea if necessary) and to vitalize the Chinese to a point where, with assistance of American air power and some supplies, they can mop out their own country.

Casualties. Our experience in the Pacific War is so diverse as to casualties that it is considered wrong to give any estimate in numbers. Using various combinations of Pacific experience, the War Department staff reaches the conclusion that the cost of securing a worthwhile position in Korea would almost certainly be greater than the cost of the Kyushu operation. Points on the opti-

mistic side of the Kyushu operation are that:
General MacArthur has not yet accepted responsibility for going ashore where there would be
disproportionate casualties. The nature of the
objective area gives room for maneuver, both on
the land and by sea. As to any discussion of specific operations, the following data are pertinent:

Campaign	U.S. Casualties Killed, wounded, missing	Jap Casualties Killed and Prisoners (Not including wounded)	Ratio U.S. to Jap
Leyte	17,000	78,000	1:4.6
Luzon	31,000	156,000	1:5.0
Iwo Jima	20,000	25,000	1:1.25
Okinawa	34,000 (Ground	81,000	1:2
	7,700 (Navy)	(not a complete count)	
Normandy (1st 30 days)	42,000	—	—

The record of General MacArthur's operations
from 1 March 1944 through 1 May 1945 shows
13,742 U. S. killed compared to 310,165
Japanese killed, or a ratio of 22 to 1.

There is reason to believe that the first 30
days in Kyushu should not exceed the price we
have paid for Luzon. It is a grim fact that there
is not an easy, bloodless way to victory in war
and it is the thankless task of the leaders to
maintain their firm outward front which holds
the resolution of their subordinates. Any irresolution on the leaders may result in costly weakening and indecision in the subordinates. . . .

An important point about Russian participation in the war is that the impact of Russian
entry on the already hopeless Japanese may well
be the decisive action levering them into capitulation at that time or shortly thereafter if we

land in Japan.

In considering the matter of command and control in the Pacific war which the British wish to raise at the next conference,[4] we must bear in mind the point that anything smacking of combined command in the Pacific might increase the difficulties with Russia and perhaps with China. Furthermore the obvious inefficiencies of combined command may directly result in increased cost in resources and American lives.

General Marshall said that he had asked General MacArthur's opinion on the proposed operation and had received from him the following telegram, which General Marshall then read:

"I believe the operation presents less hazards of excess loss than any other that has been suggested and that its decisive effect will eventually save lives by eliminating wasteful operations of non-decisive character. I regard the operation as the most economical one in effort and lives that is possible. In this respect it must be remembered that the several preceding months will involve practically no losses in ground troops and that sooner or later a decisive ground attack must be made. The hazard and loss will be greatly lessened if an attack is launched from Siberia sufficiently ahead of our target date to commit the enemy to major combat. I most earnestly recommend no change in OLYMPIC. Additional subsidiary attacks will simply build up our final total casualties."

General Marshall said that it was his personal view that the operation against Kyushu was the only course to pursue. He felt that air power alone was not sufficient to put the Japanese out of the war. It was unable alone to put the Germans out. General Eaker and General Eisenhower both agreed to this. Against the Japanese scattered through mountainous country, the problem would be much more difficult than it had been in Germany. He felt that this plan offered the only way the Japanese could be forced into a feeling of utter hopelessness. The operation would be difficult but not more so than the assault in Normandy. He was convinced that every individual moving to the Pacific should be indoctrinated with a firm determination to see it through.

Admiral King agreed with General Marshall's views and said that the more he studied the matter, the more he was impressed with the strategic location of Kyushu, which he considered the key to the success of any siege operations. He pointed out that within three months the effects of air power based on Okinawa will begin to be felt strongly in Japan. It seemed to him that Kyushu followed logically after Okinawa. It was a natural setup. It was his opinion that we should do Kyushu now, after which there would be time to judge the effect of possible operations by the Russians and the Chinese. The weather constituted quite a factor. So far as preparation was concerned, we must aim now for Tokyo Plain; otherwise we will never be able to accomplish it. If preparations do not forward now, they cannot be arranged for later. Once started however, they can always be stopped if desired.[5]

General Marshall agreed that Kyushu was a necessity and pointed out that it constituted a landing in the Japanese homeland. Kyushu having been arranged for, the decision as to further action could be made later.

The President inquired if a later decision would not depend on what the Russians agree to do. It was agreed that this would have considerable influence.

The President then asked Admiral Leahy for his views of the situation.

Admiral Leahy recalled that the President had been interested in knowing what the price in casualties for Kyushu would be and whether or not that price could be paid. He pointed out that the troops on Okinawa had lost 35 percent in casualties. If this percentage were applied to the number of troops to be employed in Kyushu, he thought from the similarity of the fighting to be expected that this would give a good estimate of the casualties to be expected. He was interested therefore in finding out how many troops are to be used in Kyushu.

Admiral King called attention to what he considered an important difference in Okinawa and Kyushu. There had been only one way to go on Okinawa. This meant a straight frontal attack against a highly fortified position. On Kyushu, however, landings would be made on three fronts simultaneously and there would be much more room for maneuver. It was his opinion that a realistic casualty figure for Kyushu would lie somewhere between the number experienced by

General MacArthur in the operations on Luzon and the Okinawa casualties.

General Marshall pointed out that the total assault troops for the Kyushu campaign were shown in the memorandum prepared for the President as 755,700. He said, in answer to the President's question as to what opposition could be expected on Kyushu, that it was estimated at eight Japanese divisions or about 350,000 troops. He said that divisions were still being raised in Japan and that reinforcement from other areas was possible but it was becoming increasingly difficult and painful.

The President asked about the possibility of reinforcements for Kyushu moving south from the other Japanese islands.

General Marshall said that it was expected that all communications with Kyushu would be destroyed.

Admiral King described in some detail the land communications between the other Japanese islands and Kyushu and stated that as a result of operations already planned, the Japanese would have to depend on sea shipping for any rein-forcement.

Admiral Leahy stressed the fact that Kyushu was an island. It was crossed by a mountain range, which would be difficult for either the Japanese or the Americans to cross. The Kyushu operation, in effect, contemplated the taking of another island from which to bring increased air power against Japan.

The President expressed the view that it was practically creating another Okinawa closer to

Japan, to which the Chiefs of Staff agreed.

The President then asked General Eaker for his opinion of the operation as an air man.

General Eaker said that he agreed completely with the statements made by General Marshall in his digest of the memorandum prepared for the President. He had just received a cable[6] in which General Arnold also expressed complete agreement. He stated that any blockade of Honshu was dependent upon airdromes on Kyushu; that the air plan contemplated employment of 40 groups of heavy bombers against Japan and that these could not be deployed without the use of airfields on Kyushu. He said that those who advocated the use against Japan of air power alone overlooked the very impressive fact that air casualties are always much heavier when the air faces the enemy alone and that these casualties never fail to drop as soon as the ground forces come in. Present air casualties are averaging 2 percent per mission, about 30 percent per month. He wished to point out and to emphasize that delay favored only the enemy and he urged that there be no delay.

The President said that as he understood it the Joint Chiefs of Staff, after weighing all the possibilities of the situation and considering all possible alternative plans were still of the unanimous opinion that the Kyushu operation was the best solution under the circumstances.

The Chiefs of Staff agreed that this was so.

The President then asked the Secretary of War for his opinion.

Mr. Stimson agreed with the Chiefs of Staff

that there was no other choice. He felt that he was personally responsible to the President more for political than for military considerations. It was his opinion that there was a large submerged class in Japan who do not favor the present war and whose full opinion and influence had never yet been felt. He felt sure that this submerged class would right and fight tenaciously if attacked on their own ground. He s concerned that something should be done to arouse them and to develop any possible influence they might have before it became necessary to come to grips with them.

The President stated that this possibility was being worked on all the time. He asked if the invasion of Japan by white men would not have the effect of more closely uniting the Japanese.

Mr. Stimson thought there was every prospect of this. He agreed with the plan proposed by the Joint Chiefs of Staff as being the best thing to do, but he still hoped for some fruitful accomplishment through other means.

The President then asked for the views of the Secretary of the Navy.

Mr. Forrestal pointed out that even if we wished to besiege Japan for a year or a year and a half, the capture of Kyushu would still be essential. Therefore, the sound decision is to proceed with the operation against Kyushu. There will still be time thereafter to consider the main decision in the light of subsequent events.

Mr. McCloy said he felt that the time was propitious now to study closely all possible means of bringing out the influence of the submerged group in Japan which had been referred to by Mr. Stimson.

The President stated that one of his objectives in connection with the coming conference would be to get from Russia all the assistance in the war that was posisble.[7] To this end he wanted to know all the decisions that he would have to make in advance in order to occupy the strongest possible position in the discussions.

Admiral Leahy said that he could not agree with those who said to him hat unless we obtain the unconditional surrender of the Japanese that we will have lost the war. He feared no menace from Japan in the foreseeable future, even if we were unsuccessful in forcing unconditional surrender. What he did fear was that our insistence on unconditional surrender would result only in making the Japanese desperate and thereby increase our casualty lists. He did not think that this was at all necessary.

The President stated that it was with that thought in mind that he had left the door open for Congress to take appropriate action with reference to unconditional surrender. However, he did not feel that he could take any action at this time to change public opinion on the matter.

The President said he considered the Kyushu plan all right from the military stand point and, so far as he was concerned, the Joint Chiefs of staff could go ahead with it; that we can do this operation and then decide as to the final action later.

*   *   *

The President reiterated that his main reason for this conference with the Chiefs of Staff was his desire to know definitely how far we could afford to go in the Japanese campaign. He had hoped that there was a possibility of preventing an Okinawa from one end of Japan to the other. He was clear on the situation now and was quite sure that the Joint Chiefs of Staff should proceed with the Kyushu operation.

With reference to operations in China, General Marshall expressed the opinion that we should not seek an over-all commander in China. The present situation in which the Generalissimo was supporting General Wedemeyer, acting as his Chief of Staff, was entirely satisfactory. The suggestion of the appointment of an over-all commander might cause some difficulty.

Admiral King said he wished to emphasize the point that, regardless of the desirability of the Russians entering the war, they were not indispensable and he did not think we should go so far as to beg them to come in. While the cost of defeating Japan would be greater, there was no question in his mind but that we could handle it alone. He thought that the realization of this fact should greatly strengthen the President's hand in the forthcoming conference.

The President and the chiefs of Staff then discussed certain other matters.[8]

[1] i.e., 3:30 p. m.
[2] Not printed herein. Text in "The Entry of the Soviet Union Into the War Against Japan: Military Plans, 1941–1945" (Washington, Department of Defense, processed, 1955), p. 76.
[3] Memorandum not printed. Apparently it was never presented to the President.
[4] See *ante*, p. 174, and *post*, p. 921.
[5] Cf. Ernest J. King and Walter Muir Whitehill, *Fleet Admiral King: A New Record* (New York, 1952), p. 605, footnote 2.
[6] Not printed.
[7] Cf. Truman, *Year of Decisions*, pp. 314–315, 322–323, 411.
[8] This paragraph may refer to discussion of a suggestion that the Japanese should be warned, before an atomic bomb was dropped on Japan, that the United States had such a weapon. See document No. 592, footnote 2.

Document 9

TOP SECRET   COPY NO. 38
J.C.S. 1338/1   (SPECIAL DISTRIBUTION)
20 June 1945
Pages 20-22, inclu.

JOINTS CHIEFS OF STAFF

PROPOSED CHANGES TO DETAILS OF THE CAM-
PAIGN AGAINST JAPAN
Reference: J. C. S. 1388

Memorandum by the commander in Chief, U.S.
Fleet and Chief of Naval Operations

FFP/A1603
Serial: 001573   20 June 1945

1.I consider J.C.S. 1388 satisfactory for purposes of discussion with the President, but consider that it should be changed in certain
respects, enumerated below, before it is given to
the President.

2. I recommend that page 7 of J.C.S. 1388 be modified as follows:

a. Change the first sentence of the first paragraph to read "By 1 March 1946 the following major naval vessels are scheduled for deployment in the Pacific:" Add to the list of vessels shown: 17 AGC (Operations and Command Headquarters Ships), 223 APA (Attack Transport Ships), 108 AKA (Attack Cargo Ships), 799 LST (Tank Landing Ships), 491 LSM (Medium Landing Ships).

DISTRIBUTION	COPY NO.
Admiral Leahy	1
General Marshall	2 & 5
Admiral King	3 & 6
General Arnold	4
General Handy	7
Admiral Edwards	8
Admiral Cooke	9
General Hull	10
General Norstad	11
Admiral Duncan	12
General Caball	13
General Lincoln	14
Captain Campbell	15
Secy, JSC	16
Secy, JPS	17
Secy, JWPC	18

b. In the fifth line of the second paragraph delete the word "constantly".

c. Modify the second and third line of the fourth paragraph to read, "all arms which are

117

required and which should be employed for the operations we contemplate are all those which can be supported."

3. Paragraph 7, page 7, on casualties is not satisfactory. Admiral Nimitz in his study of OLYMPIC has estimated that there will be 49,000 casualties in the first thirty days. It appears to me that the Chiefs of Staff will have to give an estimate of the casualties expected in the operation. As regards naval casualties I believe that a fair estimate is that they will continue at approximately the same rate as they have occurred in the Okinawa operation. The statement in paragraph 7 that the highest casualties occur during the assault phase of the operations has not, of course, been borne out in the latest operations in the Pacific where the Japanese have chosen not to defend the beaches.

4. In paragraph 11 a, page 10, the description of the Chinese Army is somewhat confusing and may leave the President in doubt as to the number of effective troops. Paragraph 11 a should emphasize that the effectiveness of any Chinese troops will be largely dependent on the assistance the United States is able to give in supplying and equipping those troops.

5. Paragraph 11 b on page 11 does not stress sufficiently what is expected of the British. He last two sentences of this paragraph should be changed to read:

"The British should continue their primary responsibility for mopping up the Japanese forces in Southeast Asia and the East Indies exclusive of the Philippines. The British Pacific Fleet and elements of the Royal Air Force and First Canadian Division mentioned above will participate in the operations for the invasion of Japan. It is the intention of the Joint Chiefs of Staff to turn over to British command certain portions of the southwest Pacific Area including Australia, the Solomons, New Guinea, New Britain, new Ireland and the Netherlands East Indies."

6. I recommend that, before the memorandum in J.C.S. 1388 is presented to the President:

a. It be amended as indicated in paragraphs 2 and 5 above.

b. The Joint Staff Planners be directed to rewrite paragraphs 7 and 11 a thereof in the light of the comments in paragraphs 3 and 4 above.

DOCUMENT 10
25 June 1945

MEMORANDUM FOR THE ASSISTANT SECRE-
TARY, WDGS:

SUBJECT: Proposed Changes to Details of the
Campaign Against Japan (JCS 1388/1)

Admiral King points out certain changes he
considers should be made in JCS 1388 and recommends:

a. Amendments be made.

b. Joint Staff Planners rewrite two of the
paragraphs in the light of his comments.

JCS 1388, which Admiral King recommends
be revised, is a proposed memorandum for the
President embodying the views of the JCS on conduct of the campaign against Japan and giving
the course of action they plan to follow. It is to be
furnished the President in preparation for the

coming conference of Heads of State.

On 18 June the President met with the JCS and Secretaries of War and Navy and, while JCS 1388 was not presented to the President, the discussion was based on it.

Since some of the changes proposed by Admiral King are not acceptable, the Chief of Staff should put his views on record in order that they may be taken into account when the Planners revise the paper. A memorandum, setting out the Chief of Staff's views and reasons therefor has been prepared for submission to the Joint Chiefs of Staff. Since this memorandum is fully explanatory, its subject matter is not repeated in these notes.

Action Recommended by OPD

Sign and dispatch the attached memorandum to the Secretary, Joint Chiefs of Staff.

Coordination

AAF

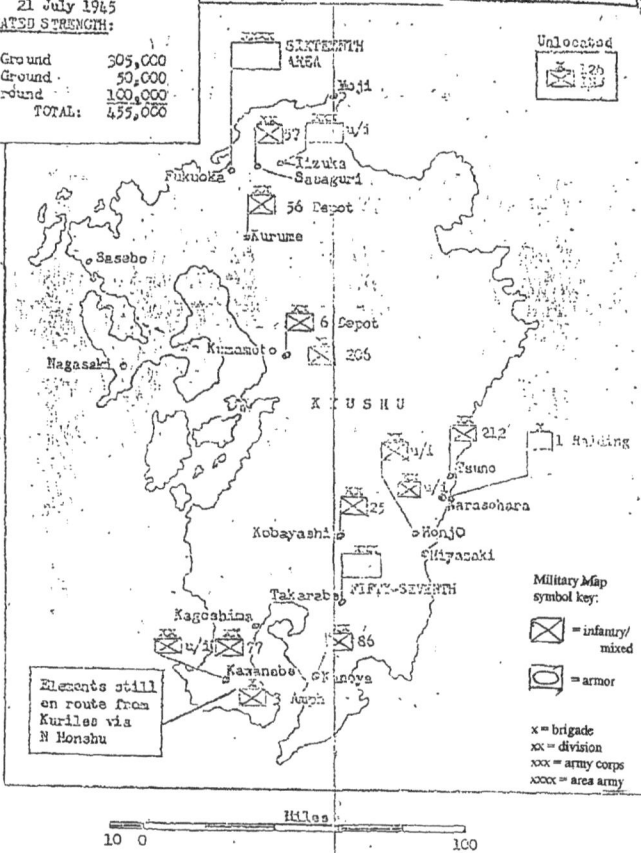

ESTIMATED
JAPANESE DISPOSITIONS
IN KYUSHU

21 July 1945
ESTIMATED STRENGTH:

Army Ground   305,000
Navy Ground   50,000
Air Ground   100,000
        TOTAL: 455,000

DOCUMENT 11

DECLASSIFIED
Authority DOD Dir 5200.1R
By OP NARA Date 1/16/8

SIXTEENTH
AREA

Moji

Unlocated
120

57   u/1
Fukuoka   Iizuka
           Sauaguri
56 Depot
Kurume
Sasebo
6 Depot
Kumamoto   206
Nagasaki
        K Y U S H U
                    212   1 Raiding
            u/1   Tsuno
            25   Narasohara
Kobayashi   Honjo
             Miyazaki
                    Military Map
Takarabe   FIFTY-SEVENTH   symbol key:
Kagoshima
u/1   77   86   = infantry/
Kananabe   Kanoya   mixed
        3 Amph   = armor

Elements still
on route from   x = brigade
Kuriles via   xx = division
N Honshu   xxx = army corps
                     xxxx = area army

                Miles
10   0   100

Note to the reader:

In the following document, the text of the second cable, "The Doctor (Gen. Groves) has just returned most enthusiastic and confident that the LITTLE BOY is as husky as his big brother," is now regarded as one of the most famous coded messages of the war. — Editor.

DOCUMENT 12
USE OF ATOMIC WEAPONS IN THE WAR
AGAINST JAPAN
No. 1303

Department of the Army Files: Telegram
*The Acting Chairman of the Interim Committee
(Harrison) to the Secretary of War (Stimson)*

TOP SECRET   WASHINGTON, 16 July 1945.
URGENT

WAR 32887. For Colonel Kyle's Eyes Only from Harrison for Mr. Stimson.
Operated on this morning. Diagnosis not yet complete but results seem satisfactory and already exceed expectations. Local press release necessary as interest extends great distance. Dr. Groves pleased. He returns tomorrow. I will keep you posted.[2]

[1] Concerning the establishment and membership of this Committee, of which Stimson was Chairman, see Stimson and Bundy, *On Active*

service in Peace and War, p. 616.
[2] Stimson's diary entry for July 16 concludes: ".
. . At 7:30 PM Harrison's first message concerning the test of the S-1 bomb arrived and I took it
at once to the President's house and showed it to
Truman and Byrnes who of course were greatly
interested, although the information was still in
very general terms." Concerning a further discussion of the message between Stimson and
Byrnes, see document No. 1236, footnote 6.

No. 1304
Department of the Army Files: Telegram
*The Acting Chairman of the Interim Committee
(Harrison) to theSecretary of War (Stimson)*

TOP SECRET   WASHINGTON, 17 July 1945.
PRIORITY

WAR 33556. TopSec Secretary of War from
Harrison.
Doctor has just returned most enthusiastic and
confident that the Little Boy is as husky as his
big brother.[1] The light in his[1] eyes discernible
from here to Highhold[1a] and I could have heard
his screams from here to my farm.[2]

[1]i.e., Fat Man.
[1a]Stimson's home on Long Island.
[2]At Upperville, Virginia.
Stimson's diary entry for July 18 includes the
following: "Harrison's second message came, giving a few of the far reaching details of the test. I
at once took it to the President who was highly

delighted. . . . The President was evidently very greatly reenforced over the message from Harrison and said he was very glad I had come to the meeting. . . ."

No. 1305
Department of the Army Files
The Commanding General, Manhattan District Project (Groves) to the Secretary of War (Stimson)

TOP SECRET   WASHINGTON, 18 July 1945.
MEMORANDUM FOR THE SECRETARY OF WAR
Subject: The Test.

1. This is not a concise, formal military report but an attempt to recite what I would have told you if you had been here on my return from New Mexico.

2. At 0530^2, 16 July 1945, in a remote section of the Alamogordo Air Base, New Mexico, the first full scale test was made of the implosion type atomic fission bomb. For the first time in history there was a nuclear explosion. And what an explosion! . . . The bomb was not dropped from an airplane but was exploded on a platform on top of a 100-foot high steel tower.

3. The test was successful beyond the most optimistic expectations of anyone. Based on the data which it has been possible to work up to date, I estimate the energy generated to be in excess of the equivalent of 15,000 to 20,000 tons of TNT; and this is a conservative estimate. Data based on measurements which we have not yet been able to reconcile would make the energy

release several times the conservative figure. There were tremendous blast effects. For a brief period there was a lighting effect within a radius of 20 miles equal to several suns in midday; a huge ball of fire was formed which lasted for several seconds. This ball mushroomed and rose to a height of over ten thousand feet before it dimmed. The light from the explosion was seen clearly at Albuquerque, Santa Fe, Silver City, El Paso and other points generally to about 180 miles away. The sound was heard to the same distance in a few instances but generally to about 100 miles. Only a few windows were broken although one was some 125 miles away. A massive cloud was formed which surged and billowed upward with tremendous power, reaching the substratosphere at an elevation of 41,000 feet, 36,000 feet above the ground, in about five minutes, breaking without interruption through a temperature inversion at 17,000 feet which most of the scientists thought would stop it. Two supplementary explosions occurred in the cloud shortly after the main explosion. The cloud contained several thousand tons of dust picked up from the ground and a considerable amount of iron in the gaseous form. Our present thought is that this iron ignited when it mixed with the oxygen in the air to cause these supplementary explosions. Huge concentrations of highly radioactive materials resulted from the fission and were contained in this cloud.

4. A crater from which all vegetation had vanished, with a diameter of 1200 feet and a slight slope toward the center, was formed. In the cen-

ter was a shallow bowl 130 feet in diameter and 6 feet in depth. The material within the crater was deeply pulverized dirt. The material within the outer circle is greenish and can be distinctly seen from as much as 5 miles away. The steel from the tower was evaporated. 1500 feet away there was a four-inch iron pipe 16 feet high set in concrete and strongly guyed. It disappeared completely.

5. One-half mile from the explosion there was a massive steel test cylinder weighing 220 tons. The base of the cylinder was solidly encased in concrete. Surrounding the cylinder was a strong steel tower 70 feet high, firmly anchored to concrete foundations. This tower is comparable to a steel building bay that would be found in typical 15 or 20 story skyscraper or in warehouse construction. Forty tons of steel were used to fabricate the tower which was 70 feet high, the height of a six story building. The cross bracing was much stronger than that normally used in ordinary steel construction. The absence of the solid walls of a building gave the blast a much less effective surface to push against. The blast tore the tower from its foundations, twisted it, ripped it apart and left it flat on the ground. The effects on the tower indicate that, at that distance, unshielded permanent steel and masonry buildings would have been destroyed. I no longer consider the Pentagon a safe shelter from such a bomb. Enclosed are a sketch showing the tower before the explosion and a telephotograph showing what it looked like afterwards.[3] None of us had expected it to be damaged.

6. The cloud traveled to a great height first in the form of a ball, then mushroomed, then changed into a long trailing chimney-shaped column and finally was sent in several directions by the variable winds at the different elevations. It deposited its dust and radioactive materials over a wide area. It was followed and monitored by medical doctors and scientists with instruments to check its radioactive effects. While here and there the activity on the ground was fairly high, at no place did it reach a concentration which required evacuation of the population. Radioactive material in small quantities was located as much as 120 miles away. The measurements are being continued in order to have adequate data with which to protect the Government's interests in case of future claims. For a few hours I was none too comfortable about the situation.

7. For distances as much as 200 miles away, observers were stationed to check on blast effects, property damage, radioactivity and reactions of the population. While complete reports have not yet been received, I now know that no persons were injured nor was there any real property damage outside our Government area. As soon as all the voluminous data can be checked and correlated, full technical studies will be possible.

8. Our long range weather predictions had indicated that we could expect weather favorable for our tests beginning on the morning of the 17th and continuing for four days. This was almost a certainty if we were to believe our long

range forecasters. The prediction for the morning of the 16th was not so certain but there was about an 80% chance of the conditions being suitable. During the night there were thunder storms with lightning flashes all over the area. The test had been originally set for 0400 hours and all the night through, because of the bad weather, there were urgings from many of the scientists to postpone the test. Such a delay might well have had crippling results due to mechanical difficulties in our complicated test set-up. Fortunately, we disregarded the urgings. We held firm and waited the night through hoping for suitable weather. We had to delay an hour and a half, to 0530, before we could fire. This was 30 minutes before sunrise.

9. Because of bad weather, our two B-29 observation airplanes were unable to take off as scheduled from Kirtland Field at Albuquerque and when they finally did get off, they found it impossible to get over the target because of the heavy clouds and the thunder storms. Certain desired observations could not be made and while the people in the airplanes saw the explosion from a distance, they were not as close as they will be in action. We still have no reason to anticipate the loss of our plane in an actual operation although we cannot guarantee safety.

10. Just before 1100 the news stories from all over the state started to flow into the Albuquerque Associated Press. I then directed the issuance by the Commanding Officer, Alamogordo Air Base of a news release as shown on the inclosure. With the assistance of the Office of

Censorship we were able to limit the news stories to the approved release supplemented in the local papers by brief stories from the many eyewitnesses not connected with our project. One of these was a blind woman who saw the light.

11. Brigadier General Thomas F. Farrell was at the control shelter located 10,000 yards south of the point of explosion. His impressions are given below:

"The scene inside the shelter was dramatic beyond words. In and around the shelter were some twenty-odd people concerned with last minute arrangements prior to firing the shot. Included were: Dr. Oppenheimer, the Director who had borne the great scientific burden of developing the weapon from the raw materials made in Tennessee and Washington and a dozen of his key assistants—Dr. Kistiakowsky, who developed the highly special explosives; Dr. Bainbridge, who supervised all the detailed arrangements for the test; Dr. Hubbard, the weather expert, and several others. Besides these, there were a handful of soldiers, two or three Army officers and one Naval officer. The shelter was cluttered with a great variety of instruments and radios.

"For some hectic two hours preceding the blast, General Groves stayed with the Director, walking with him and steadying his tense excitement. Every time the Director would be about to explode because of some untoward happening, General Groves would take him off and walk with him in the rain, counselling with him and reassuring him that everything would be all right. At t twenty minutes before zero hour, General Groves left for his station at the base camp, first because it provided a better observation point and second, because of our rule that he and I must not be together in situations where there is an element of danger, which existed at both points.

"Just after General Groves left, announcements began to be broadcast of the interval remaining before the blast. They were sent by radio to the other groups participating in and observing the test. As the time interval grew smaller and changed from minutes to seconds, the tension increased by leaps and bounds. Everyone in that room knew the awful potentialities of the thing that they thought was about to happen. The scientists felt that their figuring must be right and that the bomb had to go off but there was in everyone's mind a strong measure of doubt. The feeling of many could be expressed by 'Lord, I believe; help Thou mine unbelief.' We were reaching into the unknown and we did not know what might come of it. It can be safely said that most of those present—Christian, Jew and Atheist— were praying and praying harder than they had ever prayed before. If the shot were successful, it was a justification of the several years of intensive effort of tens of thousands of people—statesmen, scientists, engineers, manufacturers, soldiers, and many others in every walk of life.

"In that brief instant in the remote New Mexico desert the tremendous effort of the brains and brawn of all these people came suddenly and startlingly to the fullest fruition. Dr. Oppenheimer, on whom had rested a very heavy burden, grew tenser as the last seconds ticked off. He scarcely breathed. He held on to a post to steady himself. For the last few seconds, he stared directly ahead and then when the announcer shouted 'Now!' and there came this tremendous burst of light followed shortly thereafter by the deep growling roar of the explosion, his face relaxed into an expression of tremendous relief. Several of the observers standing back of the shelter to watch the lighting effects were knocked flat by the blast.

"The tension in the room let up and all started congratulating each other. Everyone sensed 'This is it!' No matter what might happen now all knew that the impossible scientific job had been done. Atomic fission would no longer be hidden in the cloisters of the theoretical physicists' dreams. It was almost full grown at birth. It was a great new force to be used for good or for evil. There was a feeling in that shelter that those concerned with its nativity should dedicate their lives to the mission that it would always be used for good and never for evil.

"Dr. Kistiakowsky, the impulsive Russian,[4] threw his arms around Dr. Oppenheimer and embraced him with shouts of glee. Others were equally enthusiastic. All the pent-up emotions were released in those few minutes and all seemed to sense immediately that the explosion had far exceeded the most optimistic expectations and wildest hopes of the scientists. All seemed to feel that they had been present at the

birth of anew age—The Age of Atomic Energy—
and felt their profound responsibility to help in
guiding into right channels the tremendous forces
which had been unlocked for the first time in history.

"As to the present war, there was a feeling
that no matter what else might happen, we now
had the means to insure its speedy conclusion
and save thousands of American lives. As to the
future, there had been brought into being something big and something new that would prove to
be immeasurably more important than the dis-
covery of electricity or any of the other great dis-
coveries which have so affected our existence.

"The effects could well be called unprecedent-
ed, magnificent, beautiful, stupendous and terri-
fying. No man-made phenomenon of such tremendous power had ever occurred before. The lighting effects beggared description. The whole country was lighted by a searing light with the intensity many times that of the midday sun. It was
golden, purple, violet, gray and blue. It lighted
every peak, crevasse and ridge of the nearby
mountain range with a clarity and beauty that
cannot be described but must be seen to be imagined. It was that beauty the great poets dream
about but describe most poorly and inadequately.
Thirty seconds after the explosion came first, the
air blast pressing hard against the people and
things, to be followed almost immediately by the
strong, sustained, awesome roar which warned of
doomsday and made us feel that we puny things
were blasphemous to dare tamper with the forces
heretofore reserved to The Almighty. Words are

inadequate tools for the job of acquainting those not present with the physical, mental and psychological effects. It had to be witnessed to be realized.'

12. My impressions of the night's high points follow:

After an hour's sleep I got up at 0100 and from that time on until about five I was with Dr. Oppenheimer constantly. Naturally he was nervous, although his mind was working at its usual extraordinary efficiency. I devoted my entire attention to shielding him from the excited and generally faulty advice of his assistants who were more than disturbed by their excitement and the uncertain weather conditions. By 0330 we decided that we could probably fire at 0530. By 0400 the rain had stopped but the sky was heavily overcast. Our decision became firmer as time went on. During most of these hours the two of us journeyed from the control house out into the darkness to look at the stars and to assure each other that the one or two visible stars were becoming brighter. At 0510 I left Dr. Oppenheimer and returned to the main observation point which was 17,000 yards from the point of explosion. In accordance with our orders I found all personnel not otherwise occupied massed on a bit of high ground.

At about two minutes of the scheduled firing time all persons lay face down with their feet pointing towards the explosion. As the remaining time was called from the loud speaker from the 10,000 yard control station there was complete silence. Dr. Conant said he had never imagined seconds could be so long. Most of the individuals in accordance with orders shielded their eyes in one way or another. There was then this burst of light of a brilliance beyond any comparison. We all rolled over and looked through dark glasses at the ball of fire. About forty seconds later came the shock wave followed by the sound, neither of which seemed startling after our complete astonishment at the extraordinary lighting intensity. Dr. Conant reached over and we shook hands in mutual congratulations. Dr. Bush, who was on the other side of me, did likewise. The feeling of the entire assembly was similar to that described by General Farrell, with even the uninitiated feeling profound awe. Drs. Conant and Bush and myself were struck by an even stronger feeling that the faith of those who had been responsible for the initiation and the carrying on of this Herculean project had been justified. I personally thought of Blondin crossing Niagara Falls on his tight rope, only to me this tight rope had lasted for almost three years and of my repeated confident-appearing assurances that such a thing was possible and that we would do it.

13. A large group of observers were stationed at a point about 27 miles north of the point of explosion. Attached is a memorandum written shortly after the explosion by Dr. E. O. Lawrence which may be of interest.

14. While General Farrell was waiting about midnight for a commercial airplane to Washington at Albuquerque—120 miles away from the site—he overheard several airport employees discussing their reaction to the blast.

One said that he was out on the parking apron; it was quite dark; then the whole southern sky was lighted as though by a bright sun; the light lasted several seconds. Another remarked that if a few exploding bombs could have such an effect, it must be terrible to have them drop on a city.

15. My liaison officer at the Alamogordo Air Base, 60 miles away, made the following report:

"There was a blinding flash of light that lighted the entire northwestern sky. In the center of the flash, there appeared to be a huge billow of smoke. The original flash lasted approximately 10 to 15 seconds. As the first flash died down, there arose in the approximate center of where the original flash had occurred an enormous ball of what appeared to be finer and closely resembled a rising sun that was three-fourths above a mountain. The ball of fire lasted approximately 15 seconds, then died down and the sky resumed an almost normal appearance.

"Almost immediately, a third, but much smaller, flash and billow of smoke of a whitish-orange color appeared in the sky, again lighting the sky for approximately 4 seconds. At the time of the original flash, the field was lighted well enough so that a newspaper could easily have been read. The second and third flashes were of much lesser intensity.

"We were in a glass-enclosed control tower some 70 feet above the ground and felt no concussion or air compression. There was no noticeable earth tremor although reports overheard at the Field during the following 24 hours indicated that some believed that they had both heard the explosion and felt some earth tremor.

16. I have not written a separate report for General Marshall as I feel you will want to show this to him. I have informed the necessary people here of our results. Lord Halifax after discussion with Mr. Harrison and myself stated that he was not sending a full report to his government at this time. I informed him that I was sending this to you and what you might wish to show it to the proper British representatives.

17. We are all fully conscious that our real goal is still before us. The battle test is what counts in the war with Japan.

18. May I express my deep personal appreciation for your congratulatory cable to us[5] and for the support and confidence which I have received from you ever since I have had this work under my charge.

19. I know that Colonel Kyle will guard these papers with his customary extraordinary care.

L R Groves

[Enclosure 3]

BULLETIN[6]

Alamogordo, N. M., July 16—William O. Eareckson, commanding officer of the Alamorgordo Army Air Base, made the following statement today:

"Several inquiries have been received concerning a heavy explosion which occurred on the Alamorgordo Air Base reservation this morning.

"A remotely located ammunition magazine containing a considerable amount of high explosive and pyrotechnics exploded.

"There was no loss of life or injury to anyone, and the property damage outside of the explosives magazine itself was negligible.

"Weather conditions affecting the content of gas shells exploded by the blast may make it desirable for the Army to evacuate temporarily a few civilians from their homes."

[Enclosure 4]
TOP SECRET
[Near Alamorgordo Air Base?], July 16, 1945.
THOUGHTS BY E. O. LAWRENCE[7]

Our group assembled at a point 27 miles from the bomb site about two in the morning. We were on a plain extending all the way to the bomb and although I did not notice carefully the mountains seemed to be some miles away. We could see in the distance lights defining the position of the bomb and at about four a. m. our radio picked up conversations between the B-29s and the ground organization.

We soon learned that zero hour was 5:30 a. m. which was just break of dawn. Naturally our tenseness grew as zero hour approached. We were warned of the probable brilliance of the explosion—so bright it would blind one looking directly at it for sometime and there was even danger of sunburn!

I decided the best place to view the flame would be through the window of the car I was sitting in, which would take out ultraviolet, but at the last minute decided to get out of the car (evidence indeed I was excited!) and just as I put my foot on the ground I was enveloped with a warm brilliant yellow white light—from darkness to brilliant sunshine in an instant and as I remember I momentarily was stunned by the surprise. It took me a second thought to tell myself, "this is indeed it!!" and then through my dark sun glasses there was a gigantic ball of fire rising rapidly from the earth—at first as brilliant as the sun, growing less brilliant as it grew boiling and swirling into the heavens. Ten or fifteen thousand feet above the ground it was orange in color and I judge a mile in diameter. At higher levels it became purple and this purple afterglow persisted for what seemed a long time (possibly it was only for a minute or two) at an elevation of 20-25,000 feet. This purple glow was due to the enormous radioactivity of the gases. (The light is in large part due to nitrogen of the air and in the laboratory we occasionally produce it in miniature with the cyclotron.)

In the earlier stages of rise of the flame the clouds above were illuminated and as the flame rose it was a grand spectacle also to see the great clouds immediately above melt away before our eyes.

The final phases was the column of hot gases smoke and dust funneling from the earth into the heavens to 40,000 feet. The column was to me surprisingly narrow until high elevations were reached when it foamed out considerably. The great funnel was visible a

[1]Stimson's diary entry for July 21 contains the following information relating to this document: " . . . At eleven thirty-five General Groves' special report was received by special courier. It was an immensely powerful document, clearly and well written and with supporting documents of the highest importance. It gave a pretty full and eloquent report of the tremendous success of the test and revealed far greater destructive power than we expected in S-1. . . .

"At three o'clock I found that Marshall had returned from the Joint Chiefs of Staff, and to save time I hurried to his house and had him read Groves' report and conferred with him about it.

"I then went to the 'Little White House' and saw President Truman. I asked him to call in Secretary Byrnes and then I read the report in its entirety and we then discussed it. They were immensely pleased. The President was tremendously pepped up by it and spoke to me of it again and again when I saw him. He said it gave him an entirely new feeling of confidence and he thanked me for having come to the Conference and being present to help him in this way."

Stimson showed Groves' report to Arnold on July 22 (see document No. 1310, footnote 3).
Concerning the discussion of the report with Churchill, see ante, pp. 203, 225.
Truman later stated that, following receipt of news that the Alamogordo test had been successful, he had called together Byrnes, Stimson, Leahy, Marshall, Arnold, Eisenhower, and King

and had asked them for their opinions as to whether the bomb should be used, and the consensus had been that it should. See Hillman, *Mr. President*, p. 248. Truman apparently also received at this meeting an oral estimate of the casualties to be expected in the assault on Japan if the new weapon were not used. See *ibid.*, and Wesley Frank Craven and James Lea Cate, eds., *The Army Air Forces in World War II* (Chicago, 1948-1958), vol. V, facsimile following p. 712 of a letter from Truman to Cate dated January 12, 1953.

[2]i. e., 5:30 a.m. All times in this memorandum are expressed in military style, i. E., from 0001 hours (12:01 a.m.) to 2400 hours (midnight).

[3]Neither reproduced.

[4]At this point is the following manuscript interpolation by Groves: "an American and Harvard professor for many years".

[5]Not printed.

[6]Identified in the source copy as a clipping from *The Albuquerque Tribune* for July 16, 1945.

[7]This memorandum, which bears an uncertified typed signature, has the following typed notation at the end: "This was written in an airplane and not corrected by the author."

DOCUMENT 13

COPY

WAR DEPARTMENT

OFFICE OF THE CHIEF OF STAFF
Washington 25, D. C.

25 July 1945

TO: General Carl Spaatz
       Commanding General
       United States Army Strategic Air Forces

1. The 509 Composite Group, 20th Air Force
will deliver its first special bomb as soon as
weather will permit visual bombing after about 3
August 1945 on one of the targets: Hiroshima,
Kokura, Niigata and Nagasaki. To carry military
and civilian scientific personnel from the War
Department to observe and record the effects of
the explosion of the bomb, additional aircraft will
accompany the airplane carrying the bomb. The

observing planes will stay several miles distant from the point of impact of the bomb.

2. Additional bombs will be delivered on the above targets as soon as made ready by the project staff. Further instructions will be issued concerning targets other than those listed above.

3. Dissemination of any and all information concerning the use of the weapon against Japan is reserved to the Secretary of War and the President of the United States. No communiques on the subject or releases of information will be issued by Commanders in the field without specific prior authority. Any news stories will be sent to the War Department for special clearance.

4. The foregoing directive is issued to you by direction and with the approval of the Secretary of War and of the Chief of Staff, USA. It is desired that you personally deliver one copy of this directive to General MacArthur and one copy to Admiral Nimitz for their information.

> /S/   Thos. T. Handy
> THOS. T. HANDY
> General, G.S.C.
> Acting Chief of Staff

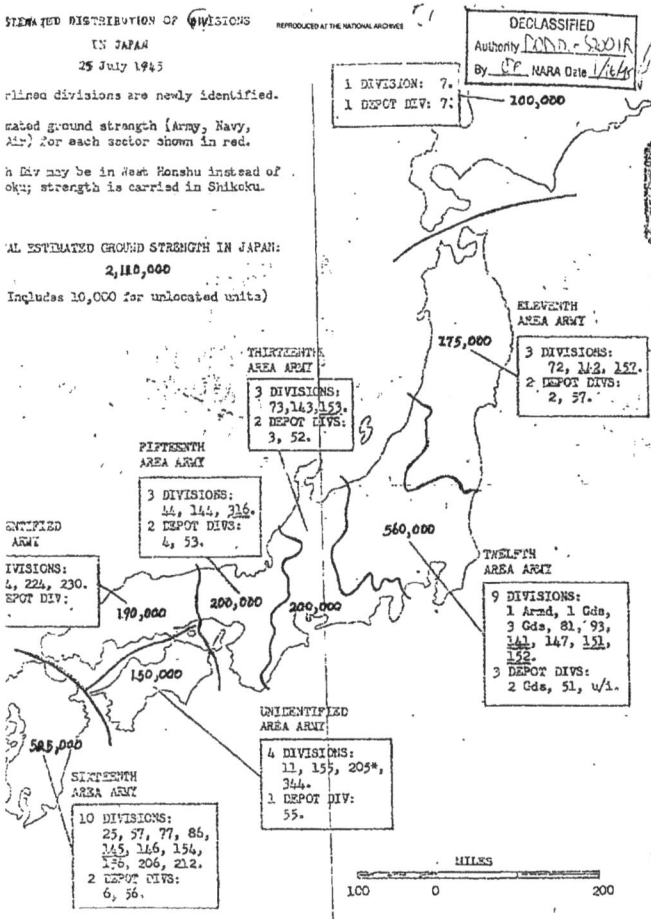

**STIMATED DISTRIBUTION OF DIVISIONS
IN JAPAN
25 July 1945**

rlined divisions are newly identified.

mated ground strength (Army, Navy, Air) for each sector shown in red.

h Div may be in West Honshu instead of oku; strength is carried in Shikoku.

AL ESTIMATED GROUND STRENGTH IN JAPAN:
2,110,000

Includes 10,000 for unlocated units)

REPRODUCED AT THE NATIONAL ARCHIVES

1 DIVISION: 7.
1 DEPOT DIV: 7.

DECLASSIFIED
Authority _____
By _____ NARA Date _____

100,000

ELEVENTH
AREA ARMY
275,000
3 DIVISIONS:
72, 142, 157.
2 DEPOT DIVS:
2, 57.

THIRTEENTH
AREA ARMY

3 DIVISIONS:
73,143,153.
2 DEPOT DIVS:
3, 52.

FIFTEENTH
AREA ARMY

3 DIVISIONS:
44, 144, 216.
2 DEPOT DIVS:
4, 53.

ENTIFIED
ARMY

IVISIONS:
4, 224, 230.
EPOT DIV:

190,000   **200,000**   **200,000**

560,000

TWELFTH
AREA ARMY

9 DIVISIONS:
1 Armd, 1 Gds,
3 Gds, 81, 93,
141, 147, 151,
152.
3 DEPOT DIVS:
2 Gds, 51, u/i.

150,000

UNIDENTIFIED
AREA ARMY

4 DIVISIONS:
11, 155, 205*,
344.
1 DEPOT DIV:
55.

585,000

SIXTEENTH
AREA ARMY

10 DIVISIONS:
25, 57, 77, 86,
145, 146, 154,
156, 206, 212.
2 DEPOT DIVS:
6, 56.

MILES

100   0   200

145

DOCUMENT 14

DOCUMENT 15

ESTIMATED
JAPANESE DISPOSITIONS
ON KYUSHU

26 July 1945
[MATED STRENGTH]:

N Ground   350,000
/ Ground   75,000
Ground   100,000
    TOTAL: 525,000

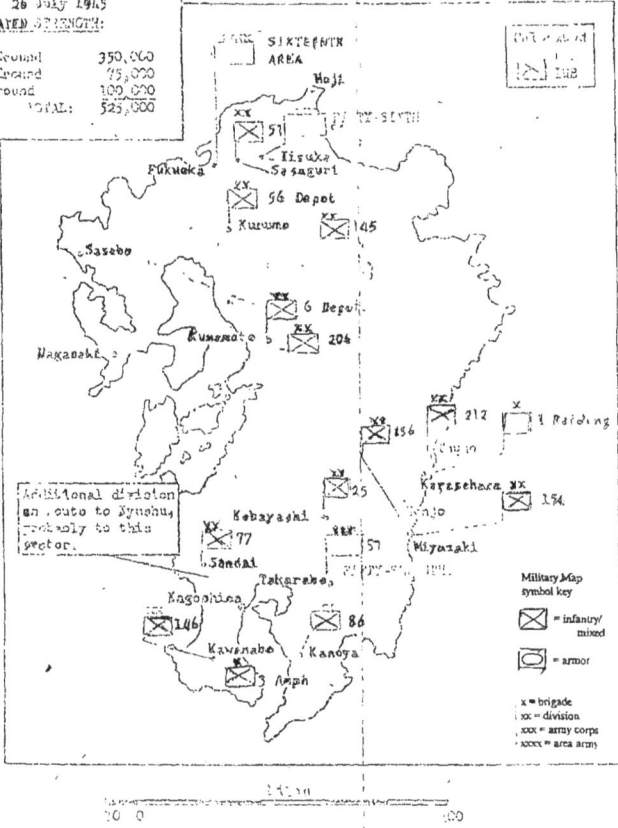

SIXTEENTH
AREA

Moji

51

Fukuoka   Iizuka
           Sasaguri

56 Depot

Kurume   145

6 Depot

Kumamoto   204

156   212   Raiding

25   Karasehara   154

Kobayashi
77   57   Miyazaki
Sendai

Kagoshima
Takarabe
146   86

Kawanabe   Kanoya
Amph

Military Map
symbol key

⊠ = infantry/
      mixed

▢ = armor

x = brigade
xx = division
xxx = army corps
xxxx = area army

Additional division
en route to Kyushu,
probably to this
sector.

10 0   100

DOCUMENT 15A

ESTIMATE OF JAPANESE AIR STRENGTH
TOTALS AS OF 26 JULY 1945

(Figures in parentheses show changes from 19 July)

1. Combat Planes:

	Army			Navy		Total	
Fighters	1235	(+131)	1306	(+ 52)	3142	(+193)	
Bombers	332	(+ 26)	820	(+ 17)	1412	(+45)	
Reconplanes	432	(+30)	173	(-2)	626	(+29)	
Floatplanes and Flying boats			593	(+ 4)	593	(+ 4)	
Total	2820	(+197)	2952	(+81)	6772	(+263)	

2. Trainers:

	Army				Total	
Advanced	1545	(+200)		1343	(+200)	
Utility	260	(+ 30)	400	620	(+ 20)	
Elementary	1900	(—)	2200	(—)	4100	(—)
Total	3705	(+230)	2500	(-)	6205	4260

DOCUMENT 16

Document 25
Papers of George M. Elsey

U.S. FOREST EUROPEAN THEATER
STAFF MESSAGE CONTROL
INCOMING MESSAGE

URGENT

FROM: AGWAR Washington

TO: Tripartite Conference Babelsberg, Germany

NO: WAR 41011   30 July 1945.

To the President from the Secretary of War.

The time schedule on Groves' project is progress-
ing so rapidly that it is now essential that statement for release by you be available not later
than Wednesday, 1 August. I have revised draft of
statement, which I previously presented to you in
light of

(A) Your recent ultimatum,

(B) Dramatic results of test and

(C) Certain minor suggestions made by British of which Byrnes is aware.

While I am planning to start a copy by special courier tomorrow in the hope you can be reached, nevertheless in the event he does not reach you in time, I will appreciate having your authority to have White House release revised statement as soon as necessary.

Sorry circumstances seem to require this emergency action.

ACTION: Gen. Vaughan

VICTORY-IN-733   (31 July 1945)   3022172
ghp:

DOCUMENT 16A

Sec War

Reply to your 4. 1011
suggestions approved
Release when ready
but not sooner than
August 2.

HST

DOCUMENT 17

TOP SECRET   COPY NO.
J.W.P.C. 397   (LIMITED DISTRIBUTION)
4 August 1945

JOINT WAR PLANS COMMITTEE

ALTERNATES TO "OLYMPIC"

Note by the Secretaries

The Joint War Plans Committee recommends that the Joint Staff Planners approve the enclosure and forward to the Joint Chiefs of Staff for their approval.
J.I.C.311 as amended and approved by the Service Members, Joint Intelligence Committee, is attached hereto as Enclosure "B".

J. T. HILLIS,
D. M. GRIBBON,
Joint Secretariat.

DISTRIBUTION   COPY NO.

Asst. Chief of Staff (Plans),
  COMINCH   1 - 2
Asst. Chief Air Staff/Plans   3 - 4
Chief, S & P Group, OPD, WDGS 5 - 6
Plans Div. COMINCH -
  Asst. Plans Officer   7
Secretary, J.P.S.   8
Secretary, J.W.P.C.   9 - 15

TOP SECRET

ENCLOSURE "A"

ALTERNATES TO "OLYMPIC"

Report by the Joint Staff Planners

1. In Enclosure "B" (page 3) the Service Members of the Joint Intelligence Committee report a considerable strengthening of Japanese forces in southern Japan proper. Along with an increase in ground units deployed in southern Kyushu, a concentration of aircraft, including the bulk of Japanese suicide aircraft, and small suicide naval craft is reported in the area.

2. The possible effect upon OLYMPIC operations of this build-up and concentration is such that it is considered commanders in the field should review their estimates of the situation, reexamine objectives in Japan as possible alternates to OLYMPIC, and prepare plans for operations against such alternate objectives.

3. The Joint Staff Planners are preparing studies of alternate objectives in the light of current intelligence estimates. These studies are to be made available to theater commanders upon completion.

4. It is recommended that the enclosed message (Appendix to Enclosure "A", page 2) be dispatched to CINCPAC and CINCAFPAC for action and to COMGENUSASTAF for information.

Enclosure "A

TOP SECRET

APPENDIX TO ENCLOSURE "A"

DRAFT

MESSAGE TO CINCPAC AND CINCAFPAC
INFORMATION TO CG, USASTAF

Copies of highly secret reports by the Joint
Intelligence Committee (J.I.C. 311, Defensive
Preparations in Japan) have been furnished you.
Report indicates strengthening of Japanese
forces and defensive measures in southern Japan
to an extent considerably in excess of that previously estimated as Japanese capability by
OLYMPIC target date. While these measures on
the part of the Japanese are not yet considered
to require change to your current directive it is
desired that you give continued consideration to
the situation particularly as it affects the execution of OLYMPIC, make alternate plans and sub-
mit timely recommendations. Operations against
extreme northern Honshu, against the Sendai
area, and directly against the Kanto Plain are
now under intensive study here.

Appendix to Enclosure "A"

TOP SECRET

ENCLOSURE "B"

DEFENSIVE PREPARATIONS IN JAPAN

Report by the Service Members, Joint
Intelligence Committee

THE PROBLEM

1. To summarize Japanese defensive prepara-
tions in the following areas:
Southern Kyushu
Northern Kyushu
Shikoku
Kanto Plain
And to determine the priorities of defense
accorded by the Japanese

GENERAL SUMMARY

2. In anticipation of Allied invasion of the
Home Islands, the Japanese are making a maximum effort to strengthen their defensive capabilities in Japan Proper and to redeploy their forces
in accordance with their own estimate of areas
most likely to be invaded. Preparations for
defense are substantiated by the following evidence: (a) ground forces are being expanded at a
greatly accelerated rate; (b) a policy of rigid con-
servation of aircraft has been adopted, new airfields constructed, and air strength is being
deployed to permit the most effective utilization

against an invading force; (c) stress is being laid upon the extensive defensive mining of approaches to threatened areas and the establishment of small craft suicide attack bases in these areas; (d) emphasis is being given to coordinated ground and air action to frustrate our landing operations supplemented by small craft and ingenious weapons to be employed in suicidal tactics. We believe that the Japanese have accorded priority for defensive preparations in the following order: (1) Southern Kyushu; (2) Shikoku; (3) Northern Kyushu; and (4) Kanto Plain. Apparently, the Japanese anticipate heavy destruction of their communication lines and are now attempting to concentrate the greatest part of the forces to be used for the defense of these vital areas in close proximity to the most threatened points of probable Allied assault.

PARTICULAR AREAS

3. There is every indication that the Japanese have been giving the highest priority to the defense of Kyushu and particularly to Southern Kyushu.

Since early 1945, ground forces deployed in Kyushu have been increased from 1 active and 2 depot divisions (totaling with army troops some 150,000 men), to a present strength of 11 active and 2 depot divisions (totalling with army troops about 545,000 men). During recent months, 2 divisions were brought in from Manchuria, 1 from Hokkaido, 2 from Honshu, and 1 from an unknown location in Japan, while 4 active divisions were formed locally from depot divisions. In addition, 1 independent mixed brigade and 3 tank brigades have been recently identified in Kyushu and one amphibious brigade has been transferred from the Kuriles to Southern Kyushu. In early 1945, about 75% of all ground forces on this island were located in Northern Kyushu, whereas now 7 of the 11 active divisions and about 60% of the total strength are deployed in Southern Kyushu.

Recent trends in the deployment of elementary biplane trainer type aircraft for suicide operations likewise point to the defensive priority which is being given to the Kyushu area by the Japanese. A total of 50 special bases for suicide aircraft are thus far known to have been designated in Kyushu, Honshu, and Shikoku west of 133° longitude. The Japanese naval air forces alone have deployed in this area 1,200 biplane trainers designated for suicide missions at the time of invasion. In comparison, only 32 such fields, 400 navy biplane trainers and 400 navy monoplane trainers have been so designated in the area between 133° and 138°, while only 22 suicide bases and 600 navy biplane trainers are thus far located in the remainder of Honshu, which includes the Tokyo Plain.

Due to their greater range and mobility, the deployment of combat aircraft is less indicative of defensive priorities than in the case of elementary biplane trainers, but it is significant that the major portion of combat aircraft in Japan Proper is deployed or scheduled to be deployed at bases west of 138° E., thus placing tactical emphasis on the Kyushu-Shikoku area.

The trend of aircraft fuel accumulations seems to be generally in line with the present and prospective deployment of combat and trainer type aircraft.

The immobilization and destruction of practically all large combatant units of the Japanese Navy has permitted the release of personnel, possibly exceeding 100,000 men for other assignments. There is evidence that many of these men from the Kure and Sasebo area will be utilized for intensifying defensive preparations in Kyushu and nearby areas. Special naval landing forces are undergoing combat training to support army ground forces in defense against Allied landings. In addition, numerous suicide attack units are being formed and trained for employment in one-man torpedoes, midget submarines, small suicide boats, and as underwater swimming teams. There is also a strong possibility that a majority of Japan's remaining destroyers will be employed in suicidal missions against our surface forces.

Many defensive mine fields have been laid and there is considerable evidence that new types of mines which might be effective against Allied landing craft are being set out in waters of less than 15 fathoms along prospective landing beaches. A very high priority has been given to the Kyushu area, the most extensive mining taking place south of 33° latitude. We believe that these mining and other naval defensive preparations in Southern Kyushu will be completed by September. Already, it is believed, an extensive mine field has been completed along the east coast of Kyushu from Tomitaka to Miyazaki. In addition, other mine fields have been laid along the approaches to Ariake Wan, Kagoshima Wan, and Tachibana Wan.

4. Shikoku. Defensive preparations in Shikoku would seem to indicate that the Japanese estimate the probability of Allied landings on this island as being second only to invasion of Kyushu or Quelpart Island.

In early 1945 no active divisions were known to be located in Shikoku, the available ground troops at that time consisting of 1 depot division and miscellaneous units totaling some 50,000 men. In recent months, however, 1 division has been brought in from Manchuria and 2 from Central and Western Honshu, and 1 active division has been created locally. Present strength, including 4 active divisions, 1 depot division and miscellaneous units, totals about 150,000 men. Recent incorporation of the ground forces in Shikoku into an area Army headquarters indicates the importance which the Japanese attach to the defense of this island.

Present deployment of the Japanese air forces, as described in paragraph 3 above, afford the Japanese equal capability for the air defense of Shikoku as compared with Kyushu. From their present bases all of the aircraft based in Japan Proper west of 138° would be within range of our assault forces attacking Shikoku.

From the naval standpoint, the Japanese are believed to have established some bases for suicide attack units in the Kochi (Lat. 33° 33' N,

Long. 133° 33' E) area. Mines have been laid in the waters along the south coast of Shikoku in the vicinity of Kochi and some of these mines may be of the shallow water type for defense against Allied landing craft approaching the beaches. Defensive minefields have also been laid in Bungo Suido between Kyushu and Shikoku.

5. Kanto Plain. While there is considerable evidence that the Japanese expect us to make initial landings in Kyushu, Shikoku or some other area of Japan Proper prior to an assault on the Kanto Plain, they do not exclude the possibility of amphibious operations against this latter area from our present positions.

In early 1945 there were only 4 active and 3 depot divisions, plus army troops totaling about 300,000 men, located in the vicinity of the Kanto Plain. Progressive reinforcement of the area has been carried out since March, 1 armored division having been brought in from Manchuria, 2 active divisions from other parts of Japan Proper, while at the same time 2 divisions were activated locally from depot divisions. Present strength in this area is estimated to be 9 active divisions, 3 depot divisions and army troops, totaling about 560,000 men. No information is available regarding any unusual recent activity in the strengthening of coastal defenses, although there is every reason to believe that here, as well as in other threatened areas of Japan Proper, fixed defenses are being constantly developed and improved.

From the air standpoint, while as stated in paragraph 3 above, there are at present only 22 special suicide bases known to be located east of 138°, it must be borne in mind that all trainer type aircraft as well as combat types based in Central Honshu would be within easy range of the Kanto Plain area. At least one large, specially concealed air base is being hastily constructed in the vicinity of Koriyama through which a large number of trainer-type aircraft could be staged, or at which 100 suicide trainers could be based. Thus, while tactical emphasis in aircraft deployment pints towards the Kyushu-Shikoku area, it is obvious that large numbers of trainer-type as well s combat aircraft will be in a position to operate effectively in the defense of the Kanto Plain.

Although some naval small craft and other suicide units have been recently formed for the added defense of this area, we believe that much less emphasis is being currently given to such defensive preparation than is the case in the general area of Kyushu and Shikoku. There is no recent information regarding the laying of additional mine fields in the vicinity of the Kanto Plain.

TOP SECRET

DOCUMENT 18

Document 54
Papers of Harry S. Truman: President's
Secretary's Files

THE WHITE HOUSE
WASHINGTON
December 23, 1952

MEMORANDUM TO GENERAL LANDRY:

Attached is a letter from Professor Cate of the University of Chicago asking clarification of the precise circumstances under which the first atomic bomb was dropped on Hiroshima.
If this letter is to be answered, it may take some research in official files and discussion with the President. Since this is an Air Force project, perhaps it would be more appropriate if you checked into this thing.
If, when the information is available, you wish us to write a reply, we will be glad to do so.

IRVING PERIMETER

Attachment

DOCUMENT 18A

THE UNIVERSITY OF CHICAGO
CHICAGO 37 o ILLINOIS

DEPARTMENT OF HISTORY
1126 EAST 59TH STREET

December 6, 1952

The President Truman
Washington, D. C.

Sir:

For several years it has been my privilege to serve as one of the editors and authors of The Army Air Forces in World War II, a history published on a non-profit basis under the joint sponsorship of the U.S. Air Force and the University of Chicago. One of my tasks for the fifth volume, now in press, was to write an account of the atomic bomb attacks against Hiroshima and Nagasaki. In respect to the decision to use the

bomb I have been faced with an apparent dis-
crepancy in the evidence which I have been
unable to resolve, and, in spite of a reluctance to
intrude upon the time of the President, I am turn-
ing to you for information for which you are the
best and perhaps the sole authority.

I have read with great interest your own
statements—that released on 6 August 1945 and
that contained in your letter to Dr. Karl T.
Compton, dated 16 December 1946 and published
in the Atlantic Monthly of February 1947. I have
read also the late Mr. Stimson's more detailed
account in Harper's Magazine of February 1947
which is in perfect accord with yours—the gist
being that the dread decision for which you
courageously assumed responsibility was made
at Potsdam "in the face of" Premier Suzuki's
rejection of the warning contained in the Potsdam
Declaration of 26 July, and that the motive was
to avoid the great loss of life that would have
attended the invasion of Kyushu scheduled for
November.

More recently I have seen a photostatic copy
of the directive to Gen. Carl Spaatz ordering him
to deliver the first atomic bomb against one of
four designated targets; the document has been
declassified and I am inclosing a true copy. The
letter is dated at Washington on 25 July 1945
and bears the signature of Gen. Thomas T. Handy,
Acting Chief of Staff during General Marshall's
absence at Potsdam. According to General
Arnold's statement elsewhere [H. H. Arnold,
Global Mission (New York, 1949), p. 589], this
directive was based on a memorandum dis-

patched by courier to Washington after a conference on 22 July between himself, Secretary Stimson, and General Marshall.

The directive contains an unqualified order to launch the attack "as soon as weather will permit visual bombing after about 3 August 1945."

There is no reference to the Potsdam Declaration which was to be issued on the next day and no statement as to what should be done in the event of a Japanese offer to surrender before 3 August. It is possible that the written directive was qualified by oral instructions, or that it was intended that it be countermanded by a radio message if the Japanese did accept the Potsdam terms, or that the directive was an erroneous representation of Secretary Stimson's real intentions. Nevertheless, as it stands the directive seems to indicate that the decision to use the bomb had been made at least one day before the promulgation of the Potsdam Declaration and two days before Suzuki's rejection thereof on 28 July, Tokyo time. Such an interpretation is in flat contradiction to the explanation implicit in the published statements, that the final decision was made only after the Japanese refusal of the ultimatum.

Because of the extraordinary importance of this problem, I am appealing to you for more complete information as to the time and the circumstances under which you arrived at the final decision, and for permission to quote your reply in the volume of which I have spoken. Your well-known interest in history has encouraged me to seek my information at the source, as the histo-

rian should, without apology other than for having intruded on your crowded schedule with a letter made overly long by my desire to state the
problem accurately.

Very truly yours,

James L. Cate
Professor of Medieval History

JLC: jm
Inclosure

DOCUMENT 18B

COPY

WAR DEPARTMENT

OFFICE OF THE CHIEF OF STAFF
Washington 25, D. C.

25 July 1945

TO: General Carl Spaatz
     Commanding General
     United States Army Strategic Air Forces

1. The 509 Composite Group, 20th Air Force
will deliver its first special bomb as soon as
weather will permit visual bombing after about 3
August 1945 on one of the targets: Hiroshima,
Kokura, Niigata and Nagasaki. To carry military
and civilian scientific personnel from the War
Department to observe and record the effects of
the explosion of the bomb, additional aircraft will
accompany the airplane carrying the bomb. The
observing planes will stay several miles distant

from the point of impact of the bomb.

2. Additional bombs will be delivered on the above targets as soon as made ready by the project staff. Further instructions will be issued concerning targets other than those listed above.

3. Dissemination of any and all information concerning the use of the weapon against Japan is reserved to the Secretary of War and the President of the United States. No communiques on the subject or releases of information will be issued by Commanders in the field without specific prior authority. Any news stories will be sent to the War Department for special clearance.

The foregoing directive is issued to you by direction and with the approval of the Secretary of War and of the Chief of Staff, USA. It is desired that you personally deliver one copy of this directive to General MacArthur and one copy to Admiral Nimitz for their information.

/S/ Thos. T. Handy
THOS. T. HANDY
General, G.S.C.
Acting Chief of Staff

DOCUMENT 18C

Document 55
Papers of Harry S. Truman: President's
Secretary's Files

THE WHITE HOUSE
WASHINGTON

30 December 1952

MEMORANDUM FOR THE PRESIDENT

Mr. President, it would be very desirable, if you could do it, to let this historian have such information as could be used in the history that he is writing concerning the circumstances under which the first atomic bombs were dropped.

R. B. LANDRY
Major General, USAF

Incl

THE WHITE HOUSE
WASHINGTON Dec. 31, 1952

My dear Professor Cate:-

Your letter of Dec. 6th 1952 has just now been delivered to me. When the message came to Potsdam that a successful atomic explosion had taken place in New Mexico, there was much excitement and consternation about the effect on the war then in progress with Japan. The next day, I told Prime Minister of Great Britain and General Ismay Stalin that the explosion had been a success. The British Prime Minister understood and appreciated what I'd told him. Prime Minister Stalin smiled and thanked me

THE WHITE HOUSE
WASHINGTON

for reporting the explosion to him but I'm sure he did not understand its significance.

I called a meeting of the Sec. of State, Mr. Byrnes, the Sec of War, Mr. Stinson, Adm. Leahy, Gen. Marshall, Gen Eisenhower, the Sec of the Navy, Adm King and some others to discuss what should be done with this awful weapon.

I asked Gen. Marshall what it would cost in lives to land on the Tokio plane and other places in Japan [It was his opinion that 1/4 million casualties would be the minimum cost as well as an equal number of the enemy.

THE WHITE HOUSE
WASHINGTON

the other military and naval
men present agreed.
I asked Sec. Stimson which
cities in Japan were devoted
exclusively to war production.
He promptly named Hiroshima
and Nagasaki, among others.
We sent an ultimatum to
Japan. It was ignored.
I ordered atomic bombs dropped
on the two cities named on
the back from Potsdam when
we were in the middle of the
Atlantic Ocean.

Dropping the bombs ended
the war, saved lives and gave

THE WHITE HOUSE
WASHINGTON

the free nations a chance
to face the facts.

When it looked as if Japan
would quit, Russia hurried
into the fray (nine days) before the
surrender so as to be in at
the settlement. No military
contribution was made by
the Russians toward victory
over Japan. Prisoners were
surrendered and Manchuria
occupied as was Korea north
of the 38th parallel.
Russia in Asia has been
a great liability since]

DOCUMENT 18E

Document 61
Papers of Harry S. Truman: President's
Secretary's Files

THE WHITE HOUSE
WASHINGTON
January 6, 1953

MEMORANDUM FOR THE PRESIDENT:

At your request I have reviewed your draft
letter to Professor Cate, and I have made a few
slight revisions after checking the details.

In your draft, you state that General Marshall
told you that a landing in Japan would cost a
quarter of a million casualties to the United
States, and an equal number of the enemy. Mr.
Stimson, in his book written by McGeorge Bundy,
says that Marshall's estimate was over a million
casualties. Your recollection sounds more reason-
able than Stimson's, but in order to avoid a con-
flict, I have changed the wording to read that

General Marshall expected a minimum of a quarter of a million casualties and possibly a much greater number—as much as a million.

Secretary Forrestal does not appear to have been at the Potsdam meetings until July 28, and your conferences about the atom bomb appear to have taken place early in the meeting, on July 22, 23 and 4. Accordingly, I have deleted the Secretary of the Navy from the list of those with whom you conferred.

I have also inserted a paragraph explaining why the orders to General Spaatz were dated July 25 rather than after the ultimatum. This has been checked with the historian of the Department of Defense.

Russian entry into the war was less than a week before the surrender.

I have deleted the last sentence of your draft, since I think that it might be unfairly used by the propagandists of the political opposition. It states a fundamental truth, but in a very restrained way, and it seemed to me that it might raise more problems than it would help.

I attach various memoranda to me on this subject from Kenneth Hechler who did the research.

DAVID D. LLOYD

DOCUMENT 18F

Document 62
Papers of Harry S. Truman: President's
Secretary's Files

THE WHITE HOUSE
WASHINGTON

January 12, 1953

My dear Professor Cates:

Your letter of December 6, 1952 has just now
been delivered to me.

When the message came to Potsdam that a
successful atomic explosion had taken place in
New Mexico, there was much excitement and
conversation about the effect on the war then in
progress with Japan.

The next day I told the Prime Minister of Great
Britain and Generalissimo Stalin that the explo-
sion had been a success. The British Prime
Minister understood and appreciated what I'd

told him. Premier Stalin smiled and thanked me
for reporting the explosion to him, but I'm sure
he did not understand its significance.
I called a meeting of the Secretary of State, Mr.
Byrnes, the Secretary of War, Mr. Stimson,
Admiral Leahy, General Marshall, General
Eisenhower, Admiral King and some others, to
discuss what should be done with this awful
weapon.
I asked General Marshall what it would cost in
lives to land on the Tokio plain and other places
in Japan. It was his opinion that such an invasion
would cost at a minimum one quarter of a million
casualties, and might cost as much as a million,
on the American side alone, with an equal number of the enemy. The other military and naval
men present agreed.
I asked Secretary Stimson which cities in Japan
wars devoted exclusively to war production. He
promptly named Hiroshima and Nagasaki, among
others.
We sent an ultimatum to Japan. It was rejected.
I ordered atomic bombs dropped on the two cities
named on the way back from Potsdam, when we
were in the middle of the Atlantic Ocean.
In your letter, you raise the fact that the directive
to General Spaatz to prepare for delivering the
bomb is dated July twenty-fifth. It was, of course,
necessary to set the military wheels in motion, as
these orders did, but the final decision was in my
hands, and was not made until we were returning from Potsdam.
Dropping the bombs ended the war, saved lives,
and gave the free nations a chance to face the

facts.
When it looked as if Japan would quit, Russia hurried into the fray less than a week before the surrender, so as to be in at the settlement. No military contribution was made by the Russians toward victory over Japan. Prisoners were surrendered and Manchuria occupied by the Soviets, as was Korea, north of the 38th parallel.

Sincerely yours,
HARRY S. TRUMAN

Professor James L. Cate,
Department of History,
The University of Chicago,
1126 East 59th Street,
Chicago, 37,
Illinois.

ABOUT THE EDITOR . . .

Thomas Fensch is the author or editor of 19 previously published books. Some of his books include:

Steinbeck and Covici:
The Story of a Friendship
Conversations with John Steinbeck
Conversations with James Thurber
Oskar Schindler and His List:
The Man, the Book, the Film,
The Holocaust and Its Survivors
Of Sneetches and Whos and the Good Dr. Seuss:
Essays on the Life and Work of
Theodor Geisel
The Man Who Was Dr. Seuss;
The Life and Work of Theodor Geisel
The Man Who Was Walter Mitty:
The Life and Work of James Thurber
Associated Press Coverage of a Major Disaster:
The Crash of Delta Flight 1141
and others . . .

He is the publisher of New Century Books and lives near Houston, Texas. He holds a doctorate from Syracuse University.

www.ingramcontent.com/pod-product-compliance
Lightning Source LLC
Chambersburg PA
CBHW030411100426
42812CB00028B/2915/J